Tim Heald is the author of the classic *The Character of Cricket* and authorised biographies of Brian Johnston and Denis Compton.

'Charming . . . Heald, biographer of the late Denis Compton, is one of the best contemporary writers on the game. His *Character of Cricket*, published a decade ago, is a joy many cricket lovers keep by their bedsides along with Wisden. This book, too, will be a delight to read in the spring, just before the season starts, to remind we flannelled fools why we bother. Equally, it will appeal even to people who are not interested in the mechanics of cricket. Heald skates over runs scored or wickets taken. He evokes time, place and, in particular, the spirit of the game to say something about the country he lives in as much as the sport he adores'
Daily Mail

'Heald is a fluent, entertaining, often graceful writer; and there is no doubting his deep affection for and knowledge of the game. There is great charm in his sketches of clubs such as Coldharbour in Surrey and Hagley in the West Midlands'
Sunday Telegraph

'Delightfully, hilariously, minutely revealing . . . what can they know of England in the summer who take no notice of the influence of this infuriating game, silly and skilful and, unlike most other English institutions, socially inclusive?'
The Times

'There is a chapter in Tim Heald's enjoyable *Village Cricket* that is worth the cover price alone . . . The truth is that "village cricket, at its best, is a mingling of abilities as well as age and class and wealth and race and everything else it's possible to mix". Tim Heald's book is a testimonial to that ideal'
Literary Review

'Highly readable . . . Heald concludes that "villages and cricket have changed more than village cricket," still a game of beery lunches and immense teas, of "two hours cricket and four in the pub," which throughout Britain thrives patchily but survives happily. Above all, the "purest of all forms of cricket" exists to remind us that anything worth doing is worth doing badly'
Word

'Those familiar with his biographies of Denis Compton and Brian Johnston will know Heald to be an agreeable presence and an elegant writer . . . He loves the names of the villages he comes across and in a nice touch composes a piece of blank verse made up entirely of some of the more evocative ones. Other rewarding digressions include a consideration of great books about village cricket'
The Wisden Cricketer

By the same author

NON-FICTION
The Character of Cricket
My Lord's (ed.)
The Duke: A Portrait of Prince Philip
Denis: The Authorised Biography of the
Incomparable Compton
Brian Johnston: The Authorised Biography
Beating Retreat: Hong Kong under the Last Governor
A Peerage for Trade

FICTION
The Simon Bognor mysteries
Class Distinctions
Stop Press
Death and the Visiting Fellow

VILLAGE CRICKET

TIM HEALD

TIME WARNER
BOOKS

TIME WARNER BOOKS

First published in Great Britain in April 2004 by Time Warner Books
This paperback edition published in April 2006

A CIP catalogue record for this book
is available from the British Library.

ISBN-13: 978-0-7515-3850-2
ISBN-10: 0-7515-3850-7

Jacket illustration: *The Cricket Match* by Maggie Rowe,
Private Collection/Bridgeman Art Library

Typeset in Bembo by
Palimpsest Book Production Ltd
Polmont, Stirlingshire

Printed and bound in Great Britain
by Clays Ltd, St Ives plc

Time Warner Books
An imprint of
Time Warner Book Group UK
Brettenham House,
Lancaster Place
London WC2E 7EN

www.twbg.co.uk

Contents

Acknowledgements

One of the pleasures of the world of cricket is the amiable and welcoming nature of its inhabitants. It's one of the things that make writing about it such fun, and ever since I first ventured onto its turf I have been overwhelmed by the generosity of people who could quite reasonably have been resentful of my trespassing. This book is a tribute to and an acknowledgement of this. Read it and you will, I hope, be able to identify those who have helped me on my way and made it possible for me to share their pleasure in cricket and all that goes with it. I would like to thank them all and I hope that, in a way, this book is a grateful letter of appreciation.

Of course it's invidious to single people out but I would like to say a particular thank you to Ben and Tim Brocklehurst, and Tim's assistant Paula Bachelor. Between them, at *The Cricketer*, they started and sustained the National Village Cricket Championship, and they were extraordinarily helpful in steering me through its labrynthine complexities and pointing me towards many of the most interesting participants. David Taylor and Laura Hill of Triple Echo Productions transformed my idea of a village cricket book into a six-part television series, and I am grateful to them not just for their enthusiasm and professionalism but also for their patience with my faltering efforts on camera.

I would also like to thank my agent Vivien Green, who sold the outline to Alan Samson at Little, Brown; and I should also thank his boss, David Young, for transferring me to the safe hands of Richard Beswick when Alan moved on. I am particularly grateful to Stephen Guise, not just for seeing the book through the production process but also for signing up Steve Dobell as my copy-editor and Paul Cox as the illustrator. Steve, Paul and I have worked together before, and it is always a pleasure and a privilege to have them on the team.

I think I should say a personal thank you to my mother, who started the whole thing off in more ways than one, and to my wife, Penelope, who, as an Australian, could be forgiven for taking a slightly condescending attitude towards English cricket but who, while triumphalist, is never truculent.

Finally I would like to pay tribute to Major Rodney. His is the only team I have ever had the privilege of captaining. Our record, over a longish period, is a modest 'Played Two, Won One, Lost One', but those two games were played in precisely the spirit in which cricket should be played. I am sure I speak for all who participated in them when I say that cricket would be the poorer without the Major and men and women like him.

Many of them can be found in the pages that follow and I thank them all.

Introduction

I have written four cricket books so far if you include *My Lord's*, which was an anthology, commissioned by E. W. Swanton himself on behalf of MCC, and the authorised biography of Brian Johnston which, like the man himself, was about more than cricket. The others were the authorised Denis Compton and an evocation of the English game called *The Character of Cricket*. This last in particular received flattering reviews and over the years it has become a sort of cult book. I know one cricket-lover who says he keeps a copy by his bed and reads it every night like a Gideon Bible.

It was terrific fun to research and write and in the decade and a half since I have never enjoyed anything more. Apart from an abortive attempt to repeat the success with golf (it failed because golf clubs were all so similar and nearly all so unpleasant!) I have never attempted a sequel, mainly because I was afraid it would be an anti-climax, but people who have enjoyed the books have, with increasing frequency, kept asking me when I was going to write another cricket book.

That was flattering too, but either other projects got in the way or I couldn't find a suitable subject – accounts of foreign cricket tours, which I would have enjoyed very much, had gone out of favour; biographical subjects had been done to death; and histories and topic-based books tended to seem insufficiently appealing to a rapidly changing and increasingly hard-nosed publishing trade.

One of the *Character of Cricket* jokes which not everyone appreciated was the chapter on a village cricket club called Trantridge Hardy. I could only include one village because the main point of the book was to look at the great county grounds. The village, like the Lancashire League Club, the Oxford Parks and the prep school at Horris Hill was little more than a token gesture. The joke was that it was a fiction. I couldn't find a single village which combined all the essential characteristics of the perfect village club and ground, so I made one up. Several angry readers protested that they had spent days combing the country in search of the place.

Even though that book was written only in 1986 it already looks like an elegy for a lost idyll. Critics, especially aficionados of the one-day game and the twenty-over thrash, maintain that the county game which I was celebrating has all but collapsed, and I'm not sure that I would now have the heart to go back and retrace my footsteps. Many true lovers of cricket feel much the same. Of course there are many wonderful features in the modern game, but that traditional county cricket I was celebrating is not in good shape. But while that game has changed almost beyond recognition the game at 'the grass roots' remains true to its essential character – or does it?

'Village' and 'cricket' are two of the most emotive words in the English language.

The village is where, in an ideal world, most of us would like to live. 'Village' says community, good neighbours, warmth, friendliness and a pervading glow of well-being. Villages are characterised by thatched cottages, roses and honeysuckles curling round their doors, by Norman churches, by Elizabethan manors and public houses called the Crown, the Garibaldi or the Something Arms. For those who believe in it the English village is Utopia.

'Cricket' in the same ideal world says stiff upper lips, straight bats on sticky wickets, fair play and 'It matters not who won or lost but how you played the game.' 'Open-air summer game played with ball, bats and wickets, between two sides of eleven players each,' says *Oxford*, missing the point which is that for those who believe in it cricket is the true English religion.

Each of the words 'village' and 'cricket' has a resonance which goes far beyond any dictionary definition. Put them together, with all their associations, and the sum is even greater than the parts. Village cricket is the very essence of Englishness.

The great historian G.M. Trevelyan explained its true and glorious significance when he wrote: 'Squire, farmer, blacksmith and labourer, with their women and children come to see the fun, were at ease together and happy all the summer afternoon. If the French *noblesse* had been capable of playing cricket with their peasants, their châteaux would never have been burnt.'

I wish that my friend and former tutor, Professor Richard Cobb, the equally great if less conventional historian of the French Revolution, were still around to argue the toss. Richard was not only a professional francophile, he also loathed cricket with a passion.

In 1986, after I had written the earlier book about cricket, Richard wrote to say that he thought it was only another of his pupils, Chris Patten (always referred to by Richard as a 'cricketer' on account of his having bowled military medium for Balliol), who, as he put it, 'went for all the Cardus stuff'.

'It was quite a shock,' Richard continued, 'to discover that you too were a cricketophile. My father used to take me to watch the beastly game – a peculiarly ENGLISH aberration (I think it would survive even under a left-wing dictatorship brought in by Labour) – generally the Kent and Sussex match at Canterbury or Maidstone, and I would turn my deck-chair away from the scene. At Shrewsbury I joined the Boat Club to escape the horrors of the hard red ball. I wonder what people see in it.'

Richard would have disagreed vehemently with Trevelyan over the causes of the French Revolution and been particularly scornful of the notion that it might have been prevented by cricket, but he would have concurred absolutely with Trevelyan's bucolic vision of 'Squire, farmer, blacksmith and labourer, with their women and children come to see the fun'. Trevelyan would not have liked Richard's description of the game as 'an aberration' but he would have agreed about its essential 'Englishness'.

For both historians the truest, most quintessentially English form of cricket was that played in the village and preferably on the village 'green'. They would both, I think, have gone further than that and argued that, like it or loathe it, cricket, and above all 'village cricket', was significant, a defining part of Englishness. Trevelyan and Cobb both evidently believed that, for better or for worse, village cricket was what set us apart from the French. And, come to that, from most of the rest of the world as well.

That's part of the thesis, but the second part of it is that neither the village nor cricket is what it was. All is woe, everywhere is decline, the golden age is dead and buried, young people today . . . and so on. Village cricket, argue the gloom-mongers, has gone the way of decency, common sense, a stiff upper lip, a straight bat and a sense of fair play. With it has gone an important part of Englishness. Without it we are not what we were.

You can get much too serious about this, and it is a fault of many of those who write about cricket, even including the universally adored Neville Cardus, that they treat the whole thing too reverentially and lyrically. It's only a game, after all. Or is it? A prime offender, in this regard, was the poet Edmund Blunden, who wrote a famous book called *Cricket Country* in 1944. I suppose, in his defence, that this purple-prosed evocation of the national game was, in part, a celebration of the gloriousness of the English against the ghastliness of the Nazi hordes. But even so.

Here is Blunden, waxing lyrical: 'I sometimes hear it proposed that cricket, the ever changeful, changeless game which some even among the English view as the prime English eccentricity, is a something to which, for thorough appreciation, a man must have been bred from the cradle or about there. If this is the truth, I qualify; for in our village and our county the game was so native, so constant, so beloved without fuss that it came to me as the air I breathed and the morning and evening.'

Not even the most ardent and rapturous cricket lover could get away with that sort of writing now. *And yet,* particularly for those of a certain age, something of this celebratory lyricism seeped into the blood. I was never completely suckered by this sort of elegiac, over-the-top belief that village cricket was the air one breathed, but I too, I confess, was brought up in the belief that there was something about Englishness which was not only unique but better, and that there was something about village cricket which contributed importantly if not definitively to this difference and this superiority.

There is enough here to define and discuss, but I never really thought to do so until one winter evening in the late nineties when I found myself speaking as guest of honour at the annual dinner of a cricket club in the far west of England.

We sat down to dinner not far short of a hundred. The men were in lounge suits, except for a couple who came in dinner jackets and black bow-ties. I never discovered who they were. There was a sprinkling of boys in their teens, maybe younger, who were completely baffled when I mentioned my biography of Denis Compton – though there was one man present old enough to have played with or at least been coached by, Denis's elder brother Leslie. The ladies wore, for the most part, frocks. No one threw as much as a bread roll. We stood to drink a toast to the Queen and her son the Duke of Cornwall. My wife presented a bouquet to a long-serving lady tea and sandwich maker who was ill and in a wheelchair.

And so on.

It would be wrong to say that dinner would have been the same a hundred years earlier. There wouldn't have been any ladies present in Victorian England, and I doubt whether the early Victorians would have dined off the sort of caterers' packed turkey dinner readily available to market-town hotels of the middling sort in the final years of the twentieth century. On the other hand there *was* a sort of time-warp quality to the event. A time traveller transported there from the nineteenth century would have felt instantly at home. Everything about the evening would have been recognisable if not identical.

However, had I written it up verbatim and set the dinner in a contemporary novel, I doubt whether my London-based editor would have accepted it. I would have been told I was betraying signs of age; that life wasn't like that any more. 'Raffle tickets?! Tea ladies? Get real!' I dare say I might have felt the same if I were still living in London. The south-east of England was in tune with reality and the present day. The event that I was describing was far too out of date and old-fashioned to be plausible. Wasn't it?

The more I thought about it, the more I wanted to know. Was the sort of old-fashioned, other-worldly innocence I felt I had caught here at the annual cricket dinner an illusion? Was I being naïve? Would I find myself in similar situations in places equally far from London? Was this atmosphere a function of distance from the big smoke?

I've often thought of cricket as a metaphor for life – a belief that invites derisive cries of 'Pseuds' Corner!', and which can, I concede, be taken too far. Yet there *is* something in it. And if there is any truth in the idea then it is at the grass-roots that it becomes truest. Here in the far west I sensed that people still played more or less in the

old-fashioned spirit, but would this be as true in Surrey, say?
Or up north, where they used to whistle fast bowlers up
from the pits and spades are called bloody shovels. Would the
women still make the sandwiches up-country?

And so on. Cue for a quest. I would write another cricket
book and try to discover the truth about village cricket in
the modern age.

1

Somerset to Open

My own original brushes with village cricket were vicarious. My father, a classic village cricketer in the sense that his batting was robust if technically impaired, his bowling fiery but erratic, and his appearances unstructured and unreliable, never talked about a cricket team in his home village of Woburn Sands in Bedfordshire. My mother on the other hand spoke often and nostalgically of the village team at Martock in Somerset where she was born and brought up.

Martock was, in the twenties and thirties a quintessential English village where my grandfather owned an ill-fated glove manufacturing business. The glorious hamstone church looks out on a fine avenue of yews originally planted by my maternal ancestors and a number of them lie in the family plot in the graveyard. The village has grown in recent years and though it hit the headlines when a local barmaid was brutally murdered, still gives the impression of being a sleepy sort of place. Crime writers since Conan Doyle and Agatha Christie have traded on this dramatic contradiction between superficial bucolic innocence and the violence that often lies beneath. Remember Conan Doyle's famous Holmesism: 'It is my belief, Watson, founded upon my experience, that the lowest and vilest alleys of London do not present a more dreadful record of sin than the smiling and beautiful countryside.' All the same I don't recall many village cricket murders. Dorothy Sayers' hero Peter Wimsey was a fine cricketer, as was E. W. Hornung's A. J. Raffles, the finest spin bowler of his generation and the most successful gentleman thief, but neither, as far as I recall, was ever involved in a specifically cricketing crime on the village green.

My grandfather Thomas Vaughan scored for Martock. I should have guessed he wasn't much of a player but that he loved the game. Those who score are like that and I fear it is in the genes. I have never been a scorer myself, but I cannot pretend that I have ever been much of a performer either, though I love the game and all that goes with it. Or most that goes with it.

'If you do shake a Martock man,' the saying went, 'you do hear the beans rattle.' Which meant that the village was famous for beans as well as gloves. It was the village greengrocer whom my aunt and mother most often and most vividly recalled from the cricket team. Apparently he would always bring a basket to cricket matches. This would be full, not of Martock beans, but of exotic fruits. The greengrocer would sit by his basket throughout the Martock innings but would pack it away while he was on the field of play. Thus it was that shortly before he went in to bat he would look around the dressing-room and cry out to his team-mates in the broadest of Somerset accents, 'Now do anybody want a bananny before I do go out to bat?'

In those days Martock had a celebrated cricketing vicar, Prebendary Wickham. Wickham, a wicketkeeper, was possibly too good a cricketer to be classified as a 'village' cricketer, and yet for me his memory evokes a strand of classic English cricket that was once a vital component of the game. Wickham's other great passion, apart from cricket, was butterflies. Before arriving at Martock he had played for Norfolk, and soon after moving south he was snapped up by Somerset for whom he played 136 innings at an average of just under ten. In those days it was perfectly acceptable for a good keeper to be a rabbit with the bat and to go in, as Wickham did, at number eleven. He was behind the stumps in 1895 when Archie Maclaren made 424 for Lancashire at Taunton and on another occasion when W.G. Grace himself made 288. Wickham subsequently claimed that the ball only passed the doctor's bat on four occasions in the entire innings.

My Aunt Betty treasured a cutting from *The Times* which described an occasion when the Vicar of Martock came to cricket's headquarters to play for the county against Middlesex. 'A peculiar picture presented itself at Lord's,' wrote the *Times* correspondent, 'in the person of A.P. Wickham, the Somerset wicketkeeper standing with legs so far apart that his head just appeared above the wicket. He looked a queer figure even without his eccentric attire. He wore white leg guards with black knee pieces. Above these were grey trousers and

a black band or sash. A white shirt and a brilliant parti-
coloured harlequin cap completed his curious "get-up".'

That day Wickham went in last and he and a man called
Nichols shared a useful stand which ensured a marginally
respectable score of over 150. 'Thanks to their plucky batting,'
wrote *The Times*, 'the score mounted and mounted, each fresh
hit being punctuated by rounds of cheering till the total
reached 157. Certainly Somerset did not fail for the lack of
enthusiastic supporters.'

I don't know if Wickham turned out for the village team.
My aunt is dead and my mother doesn't know. Whether the
late Victorian vicar did or not, his would surely have been a
benign influence. In my mind's eye every village team should
have a parson there or thereabouts, even if the nearest he
gets to the field of play is to say grace before and after dinner.
The Church in cricket has a noble tradition ranging from
cricketing bishops such as the former England captain and
Bishop of Liverpool, David Sheppard, to the fanatical Bishop
Bill Ind of Truro, who joined me and the playwright Ronald
Harwood in a cricketing panel at the Daphne du Maurier
Festival in my home town of Fowey in the late spring of
2003. In the course of my quest for the modern soul of
village cricket I did manage to turn up a real modern cricketing vicar, but they are fewer and further between than they
were when Prebendary Wickham was in his pomp. Their
decline has as much to do with the change in the Church
as the change in village life and in cricket, but it is a decline
nonetheless and one to be regretted. On Ascension Day 1976
I was watching cricket at Taunton (first sighting of Ian
Botham) with Christopher Hollis, politician, man of letters
and the son of a Bishop of Taunton no less. I lamented the
already apparent decline of the cricketing clergy. 'Fewer vicars,'

he replied laconically, which is true but only up to a point. Another friend of mine, John Tyerman Williams, author of *Pooh and the Philosophers*, wrote a doctoral thesis on parsons who rode to hounds. Not many of them around now either, and it isn't entirely because there are fewer vicars these days. It says as much about modern attitudes to hunting. And cricket too.

I have a vision of Martock cricket, even though my family has not lived there since the glove factory folded and my grandfather died young before the outbreak of the Second World War. Because it is part of my childhood and family mythology I imagine cricket being played in the same sort of time warp that I encountered at the seminal West Country cricket dinner. It was encouraging to learn – off the web, where else! – that two Martock men, Mike Sparrow and Gareth Isaac, were advertising for schoolchildren in year six and above to take part in coaching sessions with a view to forming junior Martock sides to play in the mid-Wessex Under Fourteen League. Excellent, I thought to myself, cricket in Martock is alive and well and expanding. All this talk of doom and gloom is typical depressing media rubbish based on no hard facts at all.

Then, however, I learned a horrid truth. Martock men no longer play cricket in the village. In other ways Martock, it transpired, was thriving. Old buildings and monuments had been restored, so the local hamstone gleamed. New houses abounded. In the eighties what had once been known as Matfurlong was rebranded as the Martock Recreation Ground, and a spanking new pavilion was erected on the boundary. The village had a 'Players and Pantomime Society', a bell-ringing group, a short mat bowling club, a gardening society and even a thirty-piece orchestra. A football club, a rugby club and a tennis club all perform at the Martock Recreation Ground. But there is no longer an adult cricket club.

Mike Sparrow said he remembered the cricket but thought it had died out some time in the sixties. It was sad, he conceded, but he knew little or nothing about the cricketing past and nor did anyone else that he knew of.

This was a blow, for it confirmed much of what the pessimists proclaim. The heart has gone out of village cricket, and because of that the heart has gone out of the village. Unlike other such places Martock had retained its village shop, indeed had a whole range of them. Pubs too. And the great church throve. The cricket, however, had gone. I felt the ghostly disbelief of Prebendary Wickham in his black sash and harlequin cap and the silent reprimand of Mr Alexander with his basket of fruit and the 'bananny before I do go out to bat', and of my grandfather. I wondered what had happened to his old scorebooks and was sad.

My first real sight of village cricket was in Buckinghamshire in the early fifties. I was about six years old when my parents bought a pretty red-brick cottage just outside the village of Fulmer.

My father's Army career meant that we led a gypsy-like existence during the early years of my life. In 1947, when I was three, he was posted to Malta as Brigade Major with the Royal Marines. (He was the first regular Army officer to join the Commandos.) Some of my earliest coherent memories – Karl, our very own German POW making me a toy steamroller from old tin cans; hard-boiled eggs during picnics at Anchor Bay – are from this time, but I remember no cricket. Back home in England we stayed with my aunt and uncle in Northwood, Middlesex, but I remember no cricket there either. Then my father bought or rented a flat in a mansion block at Walton-on-Thames, where I do remember my mother bowling underarm at me while I batted in defence of a tree trunk. I don't remember my father doing anything similar, partly because he was so often away with the regiment in some foreign clime, partly because even when he was at home he lacked the inclination. It was something to do with patience, I suspect. He didn't have the temperament for long spells of bowling underarm lobs at his son. I'm not entirely sure he had the necessary accuracy either.

In 1951 the First Battalion of the Dorset Regiment was posted to Vienna. I won a copy of R.M. Ballantine's *Coral Island* for something called 'General Proficiency' (I didn't know what it meant) and was taught German at 107 Mariahilfestrasse by Frau Breuer, who had a 'beloved auntie in Letchworth' and fed me on unpasteurised yoghurt with raspberry jam. I wove her a blue and yellow scarf on a loom. I don't remember any cricket.

It was after Vienna that we moved in to Holly Cottage on a bend about a hundred yards or so down Fulmer Common Drive. Pinewood Studios was just down the road and Denham not much further. This meant that there were film people in the area. Alfie Roome, the editor, was almost a neighbour and I was friendly with his daughter Deirdre. There was a wealthy local man called Colebrooke whose hobby was carriage driving and who used to drive past the cottage behind high-stepping horses with a blanket across his knees and a brown bowler hat on his head. A dalmatian trotted between the back wheels. The great cricketer Denis Compton lived nearby, between marriages, and came once to present prizes at some party in the village hall where he cut an almost absurdly glamorous figure and annoyed the boys by kissing all the pretty girls. I saw his last innings at Lord's when I was, I think, eleven years old. He was caught on the boundary by a Worcestershire player called Outschoorn. Everyone in the crowd, especially little boys, had lumps in their throats. I got his autograph at Lord's when I found him standing outside the old Tavern talking to another man whose autograph I failed to get. As I walked away a man stopped me and asked whose autograph I'd just got. 'Denis Compton's,' I said.

'You should have got the other man's,' he said crushingly.

The other man was David Lean, the film director. I suppose looking back on it he was a greater man than Denis Compton, but to an awe-struck, cricket-mad little boy he didn't seem so. And I'm not sure he does even now.

Immediately opposite Holly Cottage was the Recreation Ground, which my brother and I called the 'Wreck and Creation Ground'. It was here that the village played cricket and there that I watched.

I wish I could explain precisely what I so enjoyed about it, but perhaps part of the game's insidious appeal is that it does defy explanation. You can analyse a Beethoven symphony, a first growth claret, or even the love of one's life. It is possible to describe them in impressively lush and evocative words, but even the English language in the hands of a maestro cannot quite do justice to any of them, let alone convey precisely what it is that makes something beautiful to a beholder (or listener, imbiber or lover).

I wouldn't begin to pretend that Fulmer village cricket in those days was like great music, fine wine or human beauty, but I came if not to love it, at least to enjoy it very much. I remember nothing of the individual games, of results, of scores, or even of individuals. What I hold in my mind is a picture not unlike the one conjured up in the best of all cricket poems, that sad lament of a Lancashire exile in the south of England who recalls my Hornby and my Barlow long ago, long ago and the run-makers flickering to and fro, to and fro. And the good news is that Fulmer Cricket Club is alive and well.

This strange almost mystical charm that I remember from the Fulmer of my early childhood is part of what I hope to convey in writing this book, for when I first saw men in white with bat and ball on fresh-mown grass I was captivated.

I was too young to contemplate actually playing for the village and, in any case, like any self-respecting little boy in the fifties I had aspirations way beyond anything as humble as the village side. None of us were particularly keen to be bowlers and I don't remember anyone who wanted to be Trueman, Statham, Tyson, Laker, Lock or Wardle. We didn't even want to be Washbrook or Edrich. We all wanted to be Hutton or Compton. The most popular cricket bats were endorsed by Len Hutton for Gradidge and Denis Compton for Slazenger. (Many many years later Denis told me that he never himself used a Slazenger bat but had special light-weight ones hand-made by a craftsman in St John's Wood. I'm glad I didn't know at the time.)

Although I was twenty-one and a journalist on the *Sunday Times* by the time my parents left Fulmer, I never did play for the village. I did, however, play on the Wreck and Creation Ground. On summer days during the school holidays I would bully or cajole my brother James, four and a half years my junior, into joining me for a one-to-one cricket contest. I have to say that my recollections and those of my brother are not identical. My memory is not that I insisted on batting at all times, nor that I deliberately hit his bowling into the nettles and bushes on the fringe of the pitch, much less that I ever, even in a moment of conceivably justified anger, actually struck him – least of all with the face of the bat. My mother, whom I would normally trust to be completely impartial, seems inclined to take my brother's side in this dispute. What she does say, and on this I am inclined to agree with her, is that we invariably set off across the road wreathed in smiles and full of optimism, only to return after a surprisingly short time in foul tempers if not actual tears.

So, as far as the Wreck and Creation Ground was concerned, spectating was definitely preferable to performing.

In the autumn of 1952 I was sent to a small boarding 'preparatory school' in Somerset called Connaught House, and it was here at Bishops Lydeard that I played my happiest cricket. It was the summer of 1957 and I was thirteen years old. The village is a few miles outside Taunton on the Minehead road – or it was in the fifties. Now it is bypassed, but while through traffic has decreased there has been a massive amount of new building. The core of the village seems much the same, although the Lethbridge Arms which used to be a Starkey Knight and Ford pub is now a free house, and Lydeard House which used to be inhabited by an old woman with a spectacular ear-trumpet is now an old people's home. More old women, I suppose, but probably no ear-trumpets.

The cricket ground was in the grounds of Watts House to the west of the village. This was now the home of Connaught House School, which had been evacuated there from Weymouth during the war, after which the headmaster, Randall Hoyle, rented it from the Boles family.

The Boleses had been keen on cricket and a previous baronet, Sir Denis, had created the ground and staged famous matches graced with the presence of R.C. Robertson-Glasgow of Cambridge and Somerset, a useful fast bowler and elegant writer, author of books and correspondent for the *Observer* before the incomparable Alan Ross. 'Crusoe' enjoyed a drink and was one of cricket's depressingly large number of suicides. He was also a great-nephew of Prebendary Wickham of Martock, though only by marriage. On one occasion at Bishops Lydeard Crusoe came on to bowl after lunch and delivered a croquet ball which broke the batsman's bat. The Boleses' butler, Burgess, who was umpiring at the time, was said to be unamused though he sounds a bit of a wag himself. Crusoe said that when Sir Denis wasn't looking Burgess would pretend to trip and fall while carrying a tray of glasses. As an eighteen-year-old Robertson-Glasgow was put on to bowl by his captain, the famous Somerset and England spinner Jack White, who farmed nearby at Combe Florey. On being asked if the field was to his liking, Robertson-Glasgow spotted Sir Denis deep in conversation with the butler, whereupon he committed the 'social solecism' of shouting out, 'Up a bit, Boles!'

Crusoe later recalled, 'The abruptness and titular inaccuracy of this request caused Jack MacBryan to sit down on the grass and laugh.'

The cricket we played wasn't quite so light-hearted but it was never taken unduly seriously. In my only year in the First Eleven I bowled slowly and inaccurately, fielded with a culpable lack of attention due to day-dreaming and batted at number seven. My top score was 14, which I achieved twice, once against the staff, when I was dropped – an easy chance – by Randall Hoyle himself while still in single

figures, and once against a school called Hill Brow out on
the edge of the Somerset Levels. If a boy made 50 he was
presented with a bat. On one occasion, against St Dunstan's,
Burnham-on-Sea, the First Eleven were all out for 10 and
the Second Eleven for 11. Or vice versa. No one seemed to
mind terribly. It was fun, though, to kit oneself out in the
real long white or cream trousers, a white shirt and blan-
coed white boots with studs, and to treat one's bat with
smelly linseed oil. Mrs Hoyle's team teas, transported to the
pavilion in the back of her Commer van, were a serious treat
– hot milky tea from an urn, sandwiches with bottled 'sandwich spread' and soap-cakes, our prep school description of
mille-feuilles – puff pastry slices with jam and synthetic cream.
The importance of tea in this class of cricket can never be
overstated. We were coached by Paul Cooper, who ran the
First Eleven, told funny stories about a mouse called
Montmorency and batted in the staff match with a sawn-
down under-sized bat with which he used to slog huge sixes
into the cabbage patch.

Once a year Bill Andrews, the Somerset coach, would
bring a squad of professionals up to the nets. I thought of
this as an extraordinarily important occasion, but Paul Cooper
disabused me. 'All without exception were disasters,' he told
me, 'excellent players in their own right but clueless when
teaching small boys who hardly knew "leg" from "off" or a
long hop from a full-toss. It is no exaggeration to say they
did far more harm than good and looked at the whole business with a benign superiority.' I'm glad I knew none of this
at the time.

Some time after the Hoyles retired the school was handed
on to a new headmaster who allegedly had an affair with a
boy's mother. This indiscretion – real or imagined – is said

to have contributed to a decline in Connaught House's fortunes. There was an amalgamation with another troubled school, but even the combined schools could not survive. Randall Hoyle did not live to see the death of the rather wonderful institution he and his wife had run, but Grizel Hoyle telephoned after the final auction of the house's contents and told me that all she had managed to salvage from the wreck were the various honours boards. Would I like mine? 'Mine' was a hefty piece of black wood with two columns of names in gold paint. The first in the top left-hand corner is P.H. Shorland who, in 1923, was awarded a scholarship to Marlborough. The last in the bottom right-hand corner is mine, with an exhibition to Sherborne in 1957. This sad and eccentric trophy now hangs in the stairwell of my home in Cornwall.

Fifty years after I first went there as a little boy in short grey trousers and a blue blazer and cap Connaught House has become a health farm called Cedar Falls and, perhaps foolishly, I went back. It's still beautiful, with views of the Blackdowns, the Quantocks, Exmoor and the Mendips, but the old thatched wooden pavilion has been replaced by a functional bungaloid structure and the scoreboard has gone too, so rotten and fragile that it collapsed with a single shove. There was a notice telling visitors that 'the areas surrounding the ground are private property' and therefore out of bounds. The Cedar Falls health farm is in the old house and they have retained most of the grounds. However, the cricket ground has become the home of the village team, who used to play at Dean Court, now given over to cattle. The Ross family, who bought the estate from Sir Denis Boles's son, Jeremy, made the pitch over to Bishops Lydeard Cricket Club in return for a peppercorn rent. Mrs Pat Ross, the philanthropic benefactor, is commemorated in a pavilion plaque of 1990 as 'our president'.

Two of the Bishops Lydeard club's stalwarts, Richard Lynes and Dave Woods, sat and chatted one fine evening as the shadows lengthened over the lovely field. At least cricket was still played there. The Somerset Stragglers, a wandering side as their name suggests, could almost call it home, I was told, as they played several games there every year, and other visitors came to play from time to time. The village itself could hold its head up high, but their existence was precarious.

'Taunton's the problem,' I was told. 'The kids won't come out here. The parents won't drive them.' Until six years ago Bishops Lydeard had a youth side, but it's collapsed. The mainstay of the club, men like those I was sitting with, had reached their early fifties and would soon have to hang up their boots. In 1993 the club had almost gone under, but somehow it staggered on. The leagues, which many experts believe to have saved the game at grass-roots levels, were not all they were cracked up to be. Under the regulations clubs in the local league were required to provide new balls for every innings of every match. The regulation balls cost £16.50. That meant £33 a game. There were 24 league matches a season. So the total outlay on balls was over £700 a season. A lot of money for a village club.

No cricket at Martock. Hard times in Bishops Lydeard. Village cricket in the county of my maternal ancestors and my childhood seemed to be in disarray, but the day after the slightly disheartening Bishops Lydeard experience I drove to another part of the country for a quite different experience.

On the Bishops Lydeard evening I had originally hoped to see Palmer's Brewery play the village. Palmers is a family business based in Bridport in Dorset, birthplace of the great

Daily Express crime reporter, Percy Hoskins, who always used to tell me with great pride that Bridport not only produced him but also the hangman's rope. In fact the rope was made by the Gundry family who owned the Hyde at Walditch and built a fine real tennis court on which to entertain the Prince of Wales in the nineteenth century. Alas, the Prince never came and the court fell into disuse and got a bad battering from American tanks during the Second World War. This has now been restored, thanks in part to Cleeves Palmer, one of the family directors of the brewery.

I'm digressing, but not as much as you may think. Cleeves had been a boy at Connaught House which was, partly, why he'd been hoping to take on Bishops Lydeard on the old Boles ground. Never mind, though, the following evening his lot were due to play another evening game against a team originally alleged to be Cattistock but turning out, it subsequently transpired, to be the summer equivalent of the Dorchester Rugby Club's Third Fifteen. They were playing at North Perrott on the border with Dorset. Actually the Perrotts are so close to the border that while North Perrott is in Somerset its twin village of South Perrott is actually in Dorset.

When I told the Bishops Lydeard men that I was going to North Perrott they looked a bit disconsolate but said they wouldn't prejudice me in any way beyond saying, 'The only thing they've got in common with us is rabbits.'

I saw what they meant as soon as I parked the car. The pavilion was the first stunner. It was an enormous double-decker – the sort of building most first-class counties would be proud of. The ground itself was a match for the pavilion. It's a cliché to say that a beautifully mown cricket field is like a billiard table, but that's just what this was like. Flat as the proverbial pancake, emerald green and smooth as silk. Cleeves, who was wandering around the wicket with a bat in hand, came over and gave a quick demonstration, hitting the ball with the gentlest of taps. It sped away as if swatted by a Botham or Richards.

As a matter of fact Botham and Richards both played at North Perrott. They came with a Somerset Eleven to play a benefit match for the Somerset wicketkeeper Derek Taylor in 1978. It also marked the beginning of the village's first season in the Somerset League and Cup as well as the national village knock-out cup. Botham hit a six-laden 67. The captain that day was Tom Parkman, still very much a fixture at the club. Not just a captain but a groundsman too. In 1978 he had the Somerset skipper, Brian Rose, caught off his bowling while his brother, Jim, bowled Botham and had Richards spectacularly caught by Tony Lawrence, one-handed on the boundary.

Partly because the ground and pavilion are so splendid, the village has attracted its share of famous cricketers. The most famous local cricketing son is Vic Marks, once of Somerset and England, and latterly of the *Observer* newspaper. Ben Hollioake came here and played for Surrey Seconds after suffering a sudden loss of form. Cricket here has not been simply agricultural or rustic.

As in Bishops Lydeard, cricket was originally the plaything of the local squire. Tom Parkman himself lent me a copy of the informative local history written by his father Leslie who was head gardener on the North Perrott estate of the Hoskyns family, who for years were the North Perrott squires.

The first formal cricket was played on Rowetts, a field by the road to Chard. In those early days the players went to

away matches in John Gear's waggonette. Gear was the village
baker who also brewed his own cough-mixture. Not everyone could fit in the waggonette, so some travelled on their
bikes. It seems that the wicketkeeper, the Revd Vere
Dashwood, a vicar obviously in the mould of Prebendary
Wickham in nearby Martock, usually travelled in the team
transport even though he had his own Ford car with a fabric
hood supported by wooden stays. This meant there could be
no lingering in local pubs after play. Players dreaded the words
'Parson's playin' Saturday mind.'

At first nearly every player came from the village and many,
like the handlebar-moustached head gardener Harry Griffiths,
also worked on the estate for the Hoskyns family. Gradually,
however, as estate and village declined in population players
were recruited from elsewhere. After Rowetts was built on,
the team moved to a ground in the park where only the
four-yard-wide wicket was mown by a push mower as the
outfield was grazed by the Squire's Dorset Horn sheep.
Droppings were picked up by hand before play, and thistles
and nettles cut with a scythe. The pavilion was a shepherd's
hut.

Of course it was all primitive but it also sounds like fun.
I particularly enjoyed the account of a match between Hal
Hoskyns's Eleven and the Women's Institute in 1929. Leslie
Parkman culled an extract from the *Western Gazette*.

Hal Hoskyns's winning the toss decided to bat first,
batting left-handed using broomstick handles instead of
bats. It was evident from the start, by the packing of the
field at square leg, that the ladies intended to exploit
the leg theory to the utmost. The men fared disastrously
at the outset losing four wickets for only seven runs.

Snappy work at the wicket by Miss Eva Lane, and the fielding of Miss Flossie Matravers were features of the game, while the steady bowling of Mrs Raper, Mrs W. Broughton, Miss M. Parkman and Miss M. Russell kept the batsmen quiet for a time. Although the ladies had to stop playing owing to bad light, the result was Women's Institute 44, Mr H.W.W. Hoskyns 79. Tea was served after the match to end a very enjoyable evening.

Much of the cricket played at North Perrott in the past seems to have been a touch frivolous. There was another light-hearted match to celebrate the Queen's Coronation in 1953 between Uncle Griff's Eleven and Ralph Trask's. 'Too many lbws and bad fielding stopped play and no one could remember who won.'

Earlier on play had been brought to a halt by the Second World War. The field was ploughed up and sown with barley, while the Manor House was taken over by a school from Surrey and the young men, including Hal Hoskyns, went off to fight.

In 1946 the Hoskyns family, anxious to get back to normality – which obviously included cricket – returned the field to grass. Before doing so, however, they had the bright idea of asking American troops who had been stationed locally to level the field with their heavy earth-moving equipment. Then the square was expertly set out and seeded by Charlie Pike and Harry Bromfield, the Squire's gardeners.

Mr Hal returned from the conflict with the rank of Major and was universally known as 'The Major', just like the resident moustache in Fawlty Towers. An avid cricketer, he turned out regularly for the club and became president. He also bought a brand new Dennis mower specially for the club and allowed his men to cut the outfield and prepare the wicket in their working hours. The days of the baker's waggonette were long over, but the team bus for many years was the Major's one-ton lorry. Perhaps, after all, there is something to be said for feudalism!

For nearly twenty years the changing-room cum tea room was housed in the hut used at various times by the Squire's shepherd or for the purpose of rearing turkeys. Then in 1974 the cricketers themselves built a new pavilion. The wondrous latest edifice went up in 2000 at a cost of £200,000, the result of some prodigious fund-raising by the locals. It's a fine focus for the village, of course, but also a useful source of revenue: £100 to hire it for a wedding; £50 for an annual dinner.

I wish I could say something riveting about the match that evening, but truth to tell there was nothing very remarkable about it. Cleeves' team was billed as Palmer's Brewery, but he was the only brewer on board. The others included two farmers, a GP, an undertaker and the owner of a toyshop. The rugby players' captain was a land agent. Because they were late starting they were only able to play for an hour or two and the captains, unbothered by the fetters of any regulating bodies, agreed that play should continue until roughly 8.30 with fifteen overs a side. Purists would, I suppose, describe it as a 'limited-overs thrash'. Everyone was in whites; everyone seemed to have fun; the game was competitive but not unpleasantly so.

Afterwards, I adjourned for dinner at the Acorn in Evershot, a few miles south over the Dorset border. Precisely the sort of place to which one should repair after watching or playing village cricket. Over the meal I pondered on what dictates survival and prosperity and what leads to decline or dissolution. Why had cricket died out in Martock, stuttered in Bishops Lydeard, and prospered in North Perrott? Was it simply chance? The enthusiasm of a cricketing squire or a dedicated groundsman like Tom Parkman?

There was a parallel survival which intrigued and slightly saddened me too. At Connaught House, playing little boys' cricket half a century earlier, we had a regular circuit of rival schools against whom we played home and away. One of them was Perrott Hill, which was in the Manor House at North Perrott. Despite their desire to return to 'normality', the Hoskyns never went back to their former home, which continued to be used as a school. After the Surrey boys departed it became Perrott Hill in 1946. Now Connaught House, despite its nineteenth-century antecedents, had gone. So had such bastions of the prep school world as St Dunstan's, Burnham-on-Sea, and St Peter's, Weston-super-Mare, where John Cleese had been a near contemporary of mine. But Perrott Hill survived. It was apparently doing very well – bigger, grander than in days of yore, rather like the neighbouring cricket ground.

When I was at school in Somerset and we were confronted with an insoluble conundrum, we used to shrug and, in broad Mummerset, say, 'The answer lies in the soil.'

Perhaps so.

2

A Disaster, a Duck and a Debut for the Major

In the autumn of 1957 I moved from Somerset to Dorset, from Connaught House School to Sherborne. The transition was a genuine rite of passage. At Connaught House, with its seventy or so boys aged between seven or eight and thirteen, the prevailing atmosphere was, despite Randall Hoyle's belief in discipline and corporal punishment, essentially benign. This intimate rather cosy feeling extended to the cricket field. Because there were so few of us at Connaught House, practically everyone who had the slightest ball sense was able to play in the First Eleven, where rebukes for dropped catches, short-pitched bowling and hitting across the line, were essentially relaxed.

Sherborne did not seem like that at all. There were more than five hundred boys in the school, and the oldest were eighteen-year-old prefects who were themselves entitled to mete out corporal punishment with canes and slippers. The culture of the school was remorselessly 'gamesy' and in its essentials had scarcely changed since Alec Waugh, Evelyn's elder brother, was expelled from the Old Boys' Society for writing one of the most controversial of all public school novels, *The Loom of Youth*, during the First World War.

A sense of fear permeated almost everything, including the cricket. Competition for the school teams was fierce, and whereas I had taken it for granted at Connaught House that one would represent the school at practically everything, the reverse was true at Sherborne. Moreover the school appeared to base all its judgements on first impressions, so that it was extraordinarily difficult to switch from B to A stream in mid-career.

More than forty years after leaving the school I found myself interviewing my former housemaster on the lawn in front of the magnificent golden-stoned Abbey Church.

'I think I only saw you play cricket once,' he said, 'and you were absolutely useless. In fact I'd say you could hardly tell one end of the bat from another.' I felt this was rather a harsh verdict on one who at Connaught House had made 14 against Hill Brow and the staff, but almost worse was the fact that he thought that he had only seen me play once. Sherborne School prided itself on catering as much for the average or below-average student as the obviously talented. If that were true, surely he should have seen me more than once. Indeed he should have been helping me in the nets as often if not more than the boys who made the school's Junior Colts side. I would have needed more help than they, but whatever its public protestations Sherborne's actual efforts to help the also-rans never quite measured up. It's a natural temptation in any school to favour the gifted. More fun to teach. Sherborne, I always felt, succumbed to the temptation. Two England cricket captains had been educated at Sherborne, the raffish A.W. Carr, who had been expelled from Eton and features thinly-disguised in *The Loom of Youth*, and the Revd David Sheppard. The two men could scarcely have been less alike, but in cricketing matters they were the yardstick. We were all supposed to aspire to their standards.

There was a catch-phrase at the time, still uttered with a mixture of amusement and terror by middle-aged men who left the school many years earlier: 'beatable offence'. There were a lot of 'beatable offences', and even if the penalty for a 'slack' performance at cricket was only fielding practice next day before breakfast, I always felt that the smell of fear lay pretty heavily on the field of play.

My house, Lyon, named after a Victorian headmaster, had been created by a strange character called Alec Trelawney-Ross who had invented the 'Ginger Week'. Luckily for me these extraordinary weeks, in which *absolutely* as opposed to *almost* everything became a 'beatable offence', were gradually being phased out by the time I arrived.

In 1935 Trelawney-Ross summarised the essentials of a Ginger Week. These included the words: 'Everyone will be required to state on his honour that, unless exempted, he has done his daily quarter of an hour of "toughing up". Cold water only for washing at night. Hot baths only 5 minutes. Kipling's "If" to be known by end of week.'

'Toughing up', which presumably meant press-ups and physical jerks, was a significant phrase and it seemed to me that the main purpose of the school was to 'tough' one up in preparation for the rigours of adult life. Cricket was an integral part of this curious and largely self-defeating exercise.

There was one happy exception to this. In almost every respect cricket was seen as a fierce struggle designed to develop manliness, strength and various other now outmoded male concepts. However we did play village cricket. Real village cricket. Every house had its proper team which competed without fear or favour against the other house teams, but most, if not all, had other teams who, from time to time, bicycled off into the lush Thomas Hardy countryside round about to take on the village sides.

School House had a team called the Agriculturalists; Westcott House had the Queries. I played occasionally for the Lyon House team, the Magnets, and I remember enjoying these games. Other Old Boys to whom I have spoken remember that the aftermath of such games was an opportunity to drink beer or cider, but this wasn't the main attraction. The games were fun; the country was lovely; and nothing, for once, seemed to be a 'beatable offence'. Milborne Port, Yetminster (where the Yetties came from), Bradford Abbas, Thornford. The names sound like the chorus of a Hardy poem. I was born in Dorset and so was my father. Every time I cross the border I experience a visceral *frisson* of home-coming. There is something about the Dorset countryside which induces an animal recognition in me. It is lovely – the most urban anti-pastoralist can see that – but for me it has an extra dimension which was nurtured by those occa-sional bicycle trips from Sherborne to the villages around.

One evening in May 2003 Hugh Archer, himself a cricketer of note, held a hog-roast for fellow Old Boys of
Sherborne School in his magnificent tithe barn at Charleton
Horethorne in Somerset. There I bumped into a man called
Harry Brewer. Harry had been at School House from 1942
to 1946. Although on his own estimation he was not a particularly proficient cricketer, he was mustard-keen and had been
an enthusiastic member of the School House Agriculturalists.
After retiring as an 'Agricultural Merchant' in 1970 he signed
on as a volunteer to drive the school mini-bus which, in the
post-bicycling age, transported the Agriculturalists to away
matches. Harry mentioned the Hardyesque villages I remembered and a few more besides: Compton Chamberlayne, Steeple
Langford, Little Bredy. Just hearing him say the names made
the hair stand up on the back of my neck.

As a long-standing resident of Nether Compton, just off
the Sherborne to Yeovil Road, Harry was a long-standing
and prominent member of the local cricket club (a former
president no less) and even now, though seventy-five years
old, the club's treasurer. Until recently the club had frequently
entertained Sherborne teams such as the Agriculturalists from
various houses including my own. In recent years, however,
the custom had become extinct. Harry didn't seem entirely
sure why. It might have been something to do with Health
and Safety regs, or maybe it was 'pressure of exams'. Whichever
was the real reason, it was abundantly clear that Harry disapproved of both.

Later in the year I went to his thatched cottage at Nether
Compton, where he and his wife had lived for the previous
forty-six years. The little house was crammed with *Wisden*s
and other cricket books, including, I was pleased to discover,
several of mine which I duly signed. Cricket, including village

cricket, induces bookishness in many of its devotees and Harry was no exception. If he wasn't playing it, watching it or umpiring, he would like to be reading about it.

The Compton club was owned by a vicar, though not, alas, the Vicar of Nether or Over Compton, and also had strong squirearchical connections. With the examples I had encountered already I was beginning to sniff the makings of a thesis involving squires and vicars, but I had studied enough history to know that my evidence so far was only anecdotal. Nevertheless I was coming across enough vicars and squires to feel that they were, or had been, significant if not crucial.

In this case there was a subtle twist to the conventional pattern in that the squire and the vicar were one and the same person, namely the Revd J.M.P. Goodden, Rector of Chipstead, Surrey. Mr Goodden is the Bishop of Southwark's adviser on 'Faith in the Countryside'. His family had been in Compton House since the early eighteenth century. Like so many of the landed gentry the family had fallen on relatively hard times. Much of the estate had already been sold off, and now the big house was going too. Until recently it had been home to a butterfly farm run by the Revd Goodden's brother, open to the public and prominently advertised on the main road. Now, however, the butterflies had moved into custom-built premises and the house was being sold to a property company who were going to convert it into four luxury apartments.

This raised the matter of the cricket ground, which was currently on a sixty-year lease. The club, which is in effect the club for Over and Nether Compton, one or two other neighbouring villages and parts of Yeovil, is actually called the Compton House Cricket Club and at an Extraordinary General Meeting in June 2002 they voted to purchase the freehold. At first, the asking price was £30,000 but a reduction of £10,000 was negotiated. Now unfortunately there was a hiatus because the actual document recording the lease appeared to have gone missing. 'Shredded,' said Harry darkly. If it didn't turn up no one seemed at all sure how to proceed, with the result that much of the steam had gone out of the necessary fund-raising.

It's certainly a lovely ground. There is just enough of a slope from the mid-wicket to square-leg boundary to provide eccentricity and perhaps home advantage. The cornfield on the opposite side to the pavilion was sprouting abundantly enough to provide effective camouflage for any ball hit for six into its stalks. On the pavilion side were two great trees, an oak and a sweet chestnut. The roots and trunk were out beyond the boundary, 'not like Canterbury', but the branches hung out over the field of play. During the last match that Harry umpired a ball was hit high into the branches of the oak and became lodged there. Local rules insist that this means a six, but there was a heated exchange because the visitors felt it should only count for four. Such is the stuff of village cricket.

Compton, I should say, is undoubtedly a village club, even though it is named after a grand house and draws its members from a variety of different places. The chairman, Paul Dobson, is from Queen Camel, a village. The secretary, Mike Pearse is from Nether Compton, like Harry, the treasurer. Peter Millard, the fixture secretary whose gang mower cuts the outfield twice a week, is from Trent, where in my day Dr Fisher, the retired Archbishop of Canterbury, used to be a sort of honorary parson, in the manner of an Alec Guinness-style grandee from *Kind Hearts and Coronets*. Darren Fenner, vice chairman, who looks after the wickets, is from Yeovil, which is definitely a town. Moreover the main team's fixtures on Saturdays in the 'Nationwide Sun Awnings Dorset League' are often against towns such as Sherborne and Beaminster or the Weymouth Second Eleven. Marnhull, whom they were playing at home in May and away in July, are definitely a village. So there is a blurring at the edges.

The Second Eleven, who play on Sundays, have a more obviously village-ish set of opponents: West and Middle Chinnock, Hardington and West Coker, Ashcott and Shapwick, Compton Dundon, Montacute. Only Crewkerne could really be described as a town – a judgement confirmed by my gazetteer which says, 'Town for an agric. area 17 m SE of Taunton. Industries inc. textiles; manu. leather goods.'

Compton also have a team in the Frome Valley Evening League, which includes the villages of Sparkford, Hardington, Milborne Port (after which I once named a character in a detective novel), East Coker and Bradford Abbas. Evening matches are played over fifteen eight-ball overs a side and the bowlers are restricted to twelve-yard run-ups. There is another series of evening games against teams with names such as 'The Trent Hangovers' which are officially described as being 'for players whose keen edge of competitiveness has become slightly dulled by the passage of time'.

The hitherto thriving youth section of Under Sixteens, Fourteens and Twelves had, however, been dealt a dastardly blow, according to Harry, by Westland Helicopters. The youth team coach had defected to Westlands and taken the boys with him.

The plain hundred-year-old pavilion belongs to the land-lord and has a tea room, kitchen and licensed bar. There is a clock in the window because the league insists that all member clubs should have a visible clock, umpires for the benefit of. An honours board hangs on one wall and there is also one of those ho-ho signs asking players not to wash their muddy balls in the sink. A framed cutting from a 1972 *Western Gazette* tells the story of the famous match when rabbits were spotted just off the playing area and players from both sides abandoned play, conjured twelve-bore shotguns apparently out of thin air and went on a bunny-slaughtering spree. The oldest extant photograph is of the 1893 team, all but one in dark trousers and nearly all the front row sporting dashing moustaches. The captain, Farley, was the father of the captain of the 1951 side. There has always been a strong family tradition at Compton, though the identities of four of the 1893 team were obviously unknown as they are captioned simply 'Yeovilian'. Since then the club has built concrete block faced changing-rooms round the original lavatories and a score-box incorporating the umpires' changing-room. A machinery store houses a Massey Ferguson tractor, three gang mowers, a Benford diesel roller, three smaller mowers and a white line marker. On one edge of the square is an all-weather artificial wicket, and there is another artificial wicket in the practice net. They also have one of those old-fashioned slip-catching cradles.

Life has changed in the forty-six years since Harry came to the village. In the fifties Nether Compton alone boasted nine different dairies. In 2003 there were none. And now the Gooddens are selling the big house for posh apartments.

Yet still those great trees stand guard over the cricket green, and from the wicket you can hear buzzards in the woods and the comforting chime of the church clock. Old Colonel and Young Colonel are long dead, the Reverend Squire is selling up. Yet some things never change.

Sadly I remember no details of my career as a Sherborne

School village cricketer. In fact all I remember is a general sense of rural ease on sunny days. I like to think that it showed the local farmers and their friends that we public school boys were not as chinless and stuck-up as they supposed; and that we learned that not everyone who lived in the villages of Somerset and Dorset were local yokels or country bumpkins. It wasn't just the villages we played. I think we played the Franciscan Friars from Batcombe, though it may only have been the lay members of the community. Another regular opponent was what in those far-off days we were still allowed to refer to as the 'loony-bin'. There was a famous story that one of their team approached a Lyon House boy during the tea-break and said, 'Excuse me, I'm a tea-pot. Would you mind pouring me out?' I cannot say for certain that it's true. I hope so.

From Sherborne I went to Oxford, where the village cricket tradition was similar to that at school. The Balliol College team was called the Erratics, and I think I played for them just twice. Once was in an end-of-term match against the dons. Christopher Hill, the great historian of the seventeenth century and recently elected Master of Balliol, was bowled by a guest player, Kate Mortimer of Somerville. Kate was not only the extremely clever daughter of the Bishop of Exeter, she was also a perfectly respectable medium-paced bowler and the holder of a half-blue, which was the most the university, in those sexually unemancipated days, offered its women cricketers. Christopher, despite his Marxist historical leanings, was in other respects a surprisingly conservative traditionalist, one of whose proudest boasts was that he had scored the winning try the last time the college won Rugby Union 'Cuppers'. He was not wildly amused to be dismissed by a woman, even if she was a bishop's daughter and a half-blue.

There was a strong vein of male chauvinism running through village cricket in those days. Actually there was a strong vein of male chauvinism running through practically everything, but as the years in question were 1962 to 1965 this was changing rapidly. This was the period when women chained themselves to the railings of the Oxford Union and, thanks to my friend Maria Aitken if I remember correctly, were admitted as full members of the University Dramatic Society. In the villages of rural Oxfordshire, however, attitudes continued much as they always had done, and village cricket sides were as unamused at being confronted by a woman as Christopher Hill.

Balliol was better known for brain than brawn, but we did have one very good cricketer, the Nawab of Pataudi, later captain of India. Pataudi took a fourth in Oriental Languages but scored thirty-three first-class centuries including six in Test matches. I once played in a college football trial when 'Tiger' was centre-half. He quickly realised that I had spent a dissipated summer and was far from fit. His idea of fun was to hoof the ball far up the left wing on which I was endeavouring to play and then shout at me to chase after it. By half-time I was feeling very ill.

'Tiger', who by now had lost an eye in a car accident, played on the same Erratics side as I did when we were opposed to the village of Great Tew, the personal and amazingly dilapidated fiefdom of Major Eustace Robb. It was a very beautiful village but very run-down. The pub, the Falkland Arms, served mild beer which was fetched up from the cellar by an elderly landlady. The thatch of the decaying cottages was more green with mould and grass than straw-coloured. Major Robb and his agent claimed to be protecting the properties from predatory weekenders.

Others in the side that day included Edward Mortimer, Kate's elder brother and now Director of Communications at the United Nations, and Chris Patten, later the last Governor of Hong Kong and now Chancellor of the University. Edward, like me, was rather bad; Chris was rather good. I remember that he bowled a crisp medium pace and had the unusual ability to make the ball 'fizz' loudly in mid-flight. I did not bowl and I fielded with my customary combination of funk, ineptitude and lack of concentration. For some reason our captain that day – could it have been Bob Guy, later the gold expert at Rothschild's bank? – decided that I should open the innings, an unaccustomed position for one who had anchored the number seven slot at Connaught House. I had vaguely supposed that I would be allowed at least one 'sighter' in the style of Bernard, the great Duke of Norfolk, a passion- ately useless cricketer even on his own ground at Arundel. (The old score-books there are full of entries saying that His Grace was out for one – the single run being the gift that etiquette demanded.) I didn't even make it to one. My recol- lection is that we played on a field outside the ruined village and that the opening bowler took an exceedingly long run. I was only moderately alarmed when he crested the brow of the hill and sped towards me. Expecting the usual off- target first delivery, I naturally played no shot and was surprised and hurt when the ball not only turned out to have pitched on a good length but was also straight enough to knock over my middle stump. It was an ignominious end, or so I thought, to my cricketing career.

Great Tew incidentally were still, at the time of writing, alive and well and playing in the second division of the

Cherwell League as Great and Little Tew. As so often seems to be the case, the competing teams are a mixture of authentic villages such as the Tews and Kingston Bagpuize – where the massive-girthed Dudley used to run the pub that put on such agreeable and cheap lunches – and towns. The Tews got off to a cracking start, making 295 for 1 in their first match at home against the Oxford and Horspath. The wicket has obviously got a lot easier since my day. Things rather deteriorated after that and by mid-season they were fighting a 'basement battle' against Oxford and Bletchingdon Nondescripts. They did manage to win this by three wickets, though only after the Nondescripts conceded an interesting-sounding 56 extras.

I was wrong, though, about that sixties golden duck putting a complete end to my coarse cricket career. Admittedly there was a long interval, but in 1992 my son Alexander was made captain of the same Erratic Balliol team from which I had retired hurt (emotionally if not physically) thirty years before. In a fit of paternal nostalgia some time around Christmas when the possibility of doing such a thing seemed agreeably remote, I said I would get up an eleven and challenge him and his friends. In middle age I rather fancied myself in the role of J.C. Squire, the publisher whose team of Invalids formed the basis for A.G. MacDonell's classic cricket cameo in his book *England, their England*. Partly because there is a famous rugby fifteen which plays the Oxford University team every year under the name 'Major Stanley's', and partly because heavily moustached Corinthian majors figure so prominently in the country house and village score-books of the early years of the century, I said we'd call ourselves 'Major Rodney's Eleven'.

To give a certain substance to the conceit I composed a short bio-pic of the Major in the style of Hugh Massingberd, former obituaries editor of the *Daily Telegraph* and the man who converted the newspaper valediction into an art-form.

Of Major Rodney I know comparatively little. He claimed to have been at Sherborne, though I can find no trace of him in the school records, and he came from a long line of majors who served mostly in the Indian Army. He himself was with the First Battalion Baluchi Lancers (Rodney's Horse) and saw active service on the Frontier in the twenties. He was Combined Services Pig-sticking Champion for a record three years in succession before being invalided out of the Army after an unfortunate incident involving pigs, sticks and a brother officer.

Retiring to his native Wiltshire he took to breeding terriers but, sadly, the Rodney never really took off. He wrote frequently and angrily to the *Daily Telegraph* and was, most famously, manager of the unbeaten MCC tour of the Mediterranean – they won every fixture except for the extraordinary tied match against the Gentlemen of Egypt in Alexandria.

At the outbreak of war he enlisted in the Home Guard and was unfortunately killed on active service somewhere near Pewsey by a stray doodlebug. He was unmarried.

You get the picture.

To my surprise, chaps seemed rather keen to play for Major Rodney's Eleven. The difficulty was that I had to get together a group of players good enough to make a game of it but not so good that they would win by too large a margin. I know the second proposition seems improbable, but early intelligence from Balliol was that the Erratics were not having a good season. The only proper village left on their fixture list was Charlton-on-Otmoor and in this fixture Charlton trounced them. They also lost to the dons, narrowly, and by a huge margin to some snooty London lawyers who arrived under the impression that they were matched against Balliol's First Eleven. In the matches against the similarly erratic sides put out by other Oxford colleges Alexander's team was proving, well, erratic, though shortly before the visit of Major Rodney's the disturbing news came through that they had defeated the Trinity Triflers by two wickets. Perhaps they were not as bad as Alexander made out.

All my serious cricketing friends warned me that if I filled all eleven places with old codgers like me our fielding would be unbending and immobile. Just as the gentlemen's teams of the eighteenth and nineteenth centuries used to employ professionals to do all the arduous running about, so I ought to pick two or three players without game knees, dodgy shoulders or figures ruined by a lifetime of executive stress and lunch. I accordingly signed up my fifteen-year-old second son, Tristram, and a school friend of his called Joe Cox, who was alleged to bowl a bit and quite fast. I also called on Hemish Goonesekere, a twenty-year-old Sri Lankan from Sussex University who had been at the London Oratory School with Alexander. Hemish was a useful all-rounder who had played for the university Second Eleven, but he warned me that he might have a hangover if we played – as we were due to – on a Sunday morning and might even oversleep. I decided to take the risk.

The experts also said I must have a wicketkeeper and I knew that David Benedictus, the author of *The Fourth of June*, now working as a BBC radio producer and an old friend and former Erratic himself, had always claimed to keep wicket. On being approached he confirmed this and said he would be delighted to play. As a precaution, however, I also secured the services of Ion Trewin, the former *Times* Literary Editor who had published my biography of Prince Philip while an editor at Hodder and Stoughton. Ion had for several seasons kept wicket in the annual match between the staff and guests at the Cornish hotel where he took his holidays.

My first choice wicketkeeper, Benedictus, was fifty-three years old and this seemed a reasonable upper age limit. Now that I had a brace of wicketkeepers as well as three young things, as well as myself in the traditional Duke of Norfolk role of only semi-playing captain, I decided to fill the remaining five places with serious enthusiasts, and preferably ones who had, once upon a time, been more or less proper cricketers.

The two best of these were Mike Trotman, of the Foreign and Commonwealth Office, whose mother had played cricket for England and who himself had represented the Royal Naval College at Dartmouth and Norfolk, and my GP Mel Henry, who still played several times each summer and said he bowled very slow flighted leg-spin. He was so keen on cricket that he once took the whole summer off and attended each Test match, travelling between grounds by canal on his own narrow boat. He did, however, come into the same hangover risk as Hemish, my Sri Lankan all-rounder, because he was playing trombone at a gig on HMS *Belfast* on the Saturday night.

My last three places went to Hugh Massingberd (previously Montgomery-Massingberd), who was not only the father of the modern English obituary who claimed to have once hit Dennis Lillee for four and whom I knew to possess a particularly fine I Zingari blazer; to Steve Dobell, who had been the editor on two of my books, *The Character of Cricket* and my biography of Denis Compton, and who had played for Charterhouse Maniacs, the Carthusian equivalent of Sherborne's village cricket teams; and finally to my brother James, veteran of the Wreck and Creation Ground in Fulmer, a former member of the Lyon House, Sherborne Magnets and now headmaster of Huish Episcopi Primary School in Somerset.

I suppose the greatest surprise of the entire episode was that the whole team showed up. This was a minor embarrassment because Alexander and I had decided that at least one of Major Rodney's was bound to oversleep or develop a last-minute injury, and he therefore had Erratics in reserve. In the end we agreed to play thirteen-a-side, with my twelve-year-old nephew Ben becoming an honorary Erratic for the day.

I have the team photo before me as I write. We are a motley crew. In the front row of five I am the only one not wearing dark glasses. It was a very hot, bright day, uncharacteristic, I suppose, of the traditional English cricketing day. Joe Cox, our non-family teenager, is in green – he changed into bright yellow when his turn came to bat; Massingberd is the only one of us wearing an old-fashioned cap – a purple job denoting membership of the Butterflies, though he too changed for batting and came out wearing the red, gold and black of I Zingari. Four of us are sporting floppy white sunhats and three of us have beards.

I shall later return to the matter of team photographs, for they are telling indicators of changing styles and traditions. When my photograph of Major Rodney's Eleven appeared in the *Cricketer* magazine it did so two pages before a photograph of the Free Foresters' 1894 trip to Ireland. The Foresters are all wearing blazers and all have hats on, mainly hooped caps though two or three have straw boaters. All the Foresters are whiskered, some with a 'full-set' but most simply with ferocious late Victorian moustaches. Three are sitting cross-legged on the grass, whereas all the 'Rodneys' are on a bench or standing.

The Master's Field, where Balliol played its cricket and where I had once been humiliated at football by Tiger Pataudi, was immaculately prepared and with the wicket plumb in the middle, the ground seemed alarmingly big. I lost the toss and they elected to bat.

The convention, I'm told, is that the captain unconfident about his fielding always positions himself at mid-on. The reason for this is that at this level of play few batsman possess a credible on-drive, so you're unlikely to have anything to do except boss your team around. Not, at the time, being aware of this, I put myself at second slip. The very first snappy ball from our Sri Lankan quick caught the top edge of the Erratic opener's bat and flew straight at my head. I was just able to fend it off. Painful and slightly humiliating. I removed myself to mid-on and put Mike Trotman at second slip instead. After a quarter of an hour Hemish beat the Erratic number one and flicked off one of his bails, but that was all the luck we had for an age.

The Erratics' second wicket put on more than 70 and I began to fear a disaster when our first-change pair, the doctor and the diplomat, settled into a groove and began to take wickets. Mind you, it required courage to keep on the leg-spinner after his first over, which must have cost more than 20 and reminded me of prep school when I fielded at square leg and there always seemed to be a conspiracy between bowler and batsman to remove the top of my head with the ball.

Our catching was diabolical but their middle order was brittle. Benedictus had a stumping off Henry's loopy leg-spin; Massingberd pouched a catch after several near misses, and in the end they were all out for 136. Difficult to be more precise about what happened because their score-book was stronger on comment than statistics. Under the 'How Out' and 'Bowler' headings there was nothing as simple as 'lbw' or 'stumped'. Instead it would be 'pathetic shot, playing across line, served him right'.

The teams took tea together upstairs at trestle tables. This was the sort of team tea that I thought had gone out with Brylcreem and Harlequin caps – thick sandwiches, cup cakes, buns and strong Indian tea in massive tin teapots.

Our batting began in public school style with Harrow, Charterhouse, Eton and Sherborne, but the old boys proved flaky and were all back in the pavilion for 33, leaving the two state-educated teenagers to more than double the score. The only public school chap who fleetingly impressed was Massingberd, changed into his I Zingari, who managed one mighty heave before being easily caught essaying another. I came in at seven, my favourite Connaught House position, and managed not to get out until we had advanced to 93. I had just moved into double figures and would have scored more if one firmly hit cow-shot had not been impeded by a plastic bag which had mysteriously found its way on to the field of play in the area of mid-wicket. I would have been miffed at getting out when I did were it not for the quality of the catch. I swatted a short ball high over cover, only to see one of the two Erratic Americans run rapidly to his left from long-off and gather as good a catch as I've seen. There's a lot to be said for baseball.

The finish was interesting and competitive without being heart-stopping. I had kept back three trumps in the persons of Trotman of the FO, Goonesekere of Sussex University and the trombonish Dr Henry. The first saw us to 112 before deciding it was too hot and chancing his arm and falling to a diving catch almost as good as the one that got me. But the other two saw us home with time and wickets to spare.

'They reversed their order,' I heard an Erratic say, ruefully, which was not entirely true but not entirely false either.

The Master, Barry Blumberg, an American Nobel Prize winner and ex-Erratic, sportingly put in an appearance before hosting a little party for the college choir. Maurice Keen, the great medievalist, spotted mowing his lawn in grey flannels and braces (his house overlooked the Master's Field), invited former pupils in for tea. After the game at least half the team adjourned to the College quad for beer and talk with men in pony-tails with rings through ears and noses, cleverer than us and young enough to be our sons – which, of course, they sometimes were.

'Don't get me wrong,' said Dr Henry, as we left through the back gate, 'but I expected more cravats . . . and boaters.'

'Not that sort of college,' I said. 'Never was. Not really.'

But the day had had a timeless quality which was almost all to do with that extraordinary game which is so eminently worth doing less than wonderfully. I like to think that much the same match could have been played fifty years ago and fifty years hence and maybe a hundred years ditto.

When the *Cricketer* published my account of this less than epic encounter at the behest of no less a cricketing God than the legendary E.W. 'Jim' Swanton, the voice of the *Daily*

Telegraph and the BBC as well as founder of his own wandering club, the Arabs, I wrote:

> There is a moral here somewhere and it does have to do with the importance of doing things badly, of being prepared to lose face, of mucking in, of playing a straight bat but not too straight, of mixing up different generations, not judging a man by the absurdity of his hooped cap or the length of his pony-tail, of clapping one's opponents on and off the field at all times and, oh, much else besides. The whole experience was oddly reassuring for more than one of us, an affirmation that change though it does there is still a little piece of England which is still England, our England, perverse, eclectic, hopeless but ultimately, despite everything, just about all right.

That should have been the last hurrah for Major Rodney. I enjoyed the day so much that I dared not risk a repeat. However, fate in the person of Carlton TV intervened a decade later.

But that is another story for another chapter.

3

A Literary Hat-trick

The more I considered writing about cricket the more I reflected on reading about it. Some of my earliest ideas and prejudices about the game were formed by the printed word. It might not be too fanciful to claim that I have enjoyed reading about cricket as much as I have enjoyed playing it or watching it, but I'm not sure. Armchair cricket of the sort involving a good book, a log fire and a glass of malt whisky is a seductive thought. And as far as village cricket is concerned its literature is as entertaining and informative as the real thing. Possibly even more fun than the actuality.

The relationship between writing and cricket is unique. No other sport has provoked so many words and, in particular, words between hard covers.

The almost impossibly erudite Professor Eric Midwinter, extrapolating from a 1964 John Arlott assessment which put the total number of published cricket books at about eight thousand, believes that we are now past the ten thousand mark. In 1950 Gerald Brodribb produced a report on 'Cricket in Fiction' which identified forty-seven novels dealing entirely with cricket and another ninety-six which included 'elements or episodes of cricket'. And there was much else besides in the form of short stories, school stories and boys' own stories. Even Prof. Midwinter fails to notice a fictional cricket match of mine in a whodunnit called *Just Desserts*. This led to several American publishers turning it down. Finally the distinguished old New York House of Scribner and Sons took it on. The editor in charge of crime, the redoubtable Rosemary Macomber, asked why I thought she'd accepted it. When I was nonplussed, she replied, 'Because of that adorable cricket match.'

I remain perplexed by this transatlantic reaction.

You would expect the relationship between cricket and words to reflect the quality of the performance, but actually you could almost argue the reverse. No, all right. V.S. Naipaul's day-by-day account of the West Indies versus England Lord's Test match of 1963 is a fine piece of reportage by a Nobel prize-winning novelist; Harold Pinter's monograph on the Somerset seamer and slogger, Arthur Wellard, is a classic of its kind; C.L.R. James's *Beyond a Boundary* is regarded by cognoscenti as the best cricket book ever written, though it transcends the differentials between 'good' (first-class, international) cricket and 'bad' (grass-roots, village) cricket.

These, however, are exceptions which prove the rule, and the rule – Heald's Law, if you like – is that the quality of prose varies in inverse proportion to the quality of the cricket. It follows from this that the best cricket literature is about indifferent performances by untalented players. This, incidentally, echoes the belief of J.M. Barrie, author of *Peter Pan*, who believed that the more distinguished a writer's prose the worse his cricket. Barrie himself, founder and captain of a famous writers' wandering cricket club, the Allahakbarries, should have known because he appears to be a case in point.

The literature of cricket has always played an important part in my love of the game. I'm not sure I don't prefer reading about it to watching it or playing it. When I first came to appreciate the game, as a boy in the fifties, I read about it in the papers – Crawford White in the *Express*, E.W. Swanton in the *Telegraph* and, of course, squads of workaday cricket hacks in *Wisden*. But with the greatest respect to the writers who featured in the newspapers and in the great *Almanack* they weren't writing what you'd describe as literature.

Even at the time, although I got an odd thrill from reading about feats of derring-do at Trent Bridge, Lord's, Old Trafford and the Oval, I got more of a buzz from a different sort of writing. Even the best of the specialist cricket writers were on the journeyman side. Fair enough, but even then you couldn't help feeling that they didn't always rise to the occasion.

One of the most exciting performances during my childhood was Jim Laker's feat in 1956 when he took nineteen Australian wickets for 90 at Old Trafford. I remember it vividly because I was on the way to join my parents in Canada – a small boy with a blue prep school cap and a Gunn and Moore bat under one arm. I flew out on a BOAC

Stratocruiser after spending the night with my uncle and aunt in Moor Park, an outer suburb in Hertfordshire. When we left for Heathrow, Australia were 112 for 2 and looked perfectly safe. As our aircraft taxied out on to the runway, however, the Captain came on the Tannoy with the news that the sun had come out and Laker and Lock were spinning the ball prodigiously. Almost at once wickets began to fall and the Captain – he must have been called Charters or Caldicot and would surely, in the movie, have been played by Basil Radford or Naunton Wayne in the style of *The Lady Vanishes* – gave us a running commentary over the Tannoy. For a little boy who loved cricket these were magic moments.

This is how Neville Cardus, widely regarded as the greatest of all cricket writers, recorded Laker's triumphs in *Wisden*: 'Against the Australians in 1956, J.C. Laker bowled himself to a prominence which might seem legendary if there were no statistics to prove that his skill did indeed perform results and deeds hitherto not considered within the range of any cricketer, living or dead.'

Cardus seems to have known that this was the literary equivalent of Bill Lawry or Geoff Boycott on a slow day, because in the next paragraph he wrote:

No writer of boy's fiction would so strain romantic credulity as to make his hero, playing for England against Australia, capture nine first-innings wickets; then help himself to all ten in the second innings. Altogether, 19 for 90 in a Test match. If any author expected us to believe that his hero was not only capable in one chapter of a marvel as fantastic as all this, but also in another chapter, and our earlier chapter, bowled a whole

Australian XI out, 10 for 88, the most gullible of his readers would, not without reason, throw the book away and wonder what the said author was taking him for.

It is almost as if Cardus knew that his prose style was not up to the challenge and decided not even to attempt to bowl properly.

Perhaps Charles Dickens is an unfair comparison but it was Dickens I was reading alongside the cricket reporters in that joyously dramatic, and winning, summer of 1956 when I was just twelve years old and all, or nearly all, was right with the world. (The Suez Crisis was a bit of a downer, but that came, mercifully, after the end of the cricket season.)

I read avidly in those days; forty or so books in a term and proper books. No Readers Digested versions or Enid Blytons. Like my friends I would sit in the classrooms we called 'The First and Second' on a summer evening, looking out on the lawn and the three great copper beeches with the ha-ha and the park beyond. I suppose there was nothing else to do, but the truth was that there was nothing else we would rather do than immerse ourselves in long, warm comfortable books by authors such as Dickens or Scott. And one of the books I wallowed in was the *Pickwick Papers* – all 640 pages of it. And the passage I enjoyed above all was the cricket match between All-Muggleton and Dingley Dell.

I have always thought of this as a classic village cricket match – *the* classic village cricket match in fact – but on returning to the original I find that All-Muggleton would have been thrown out of the *Cricketer*'s national village competition on the same grounds as poor Usk once was. Muggleton was not a village in the literal sense, for as Dickens tells us, 'Everybody whose genius has a topographical bent knows perfectly well that Muggleton is a corporate town, with a mayor, burgesses, and freemen.' So that's incontrovertible. Dingley Dell on the other hand is clearly a village. And the game they are playing is, to my way of thinking, definitely 'village' cricket.

What is immediately apparent on re-reading the account of the match is that Dickens didn't know any more about cricket than Pickwick himself. Indeed his view of the matter and of sport in general seems to be remarkably similar. When asked if he'd like to see the match Pickwick replies, 'I, sir, am delighted to view any sports which may be safely indulged in and which the impotent effects of miskilful people do not endanger human life.' (There has, you will remember, just been an unfortunate accident involving Mr Winkle, a gun, a pigeon and a crow.)

Pickwick, in other words, is one of nature's natural spectators. Professor Midwinter, in a characteristically erudite volume, called *Quill on Willow – Cricket in Literature*, reports that at cricket matches Dickens tended to be an umpire, at billiards an observer and only at croquet an occasional participant. In fact we know that there are two paintings of Dickens at cricket, one of which shows him bowling the first ball in a charity match and the other of which shows him scoring.

Back to All-Muggleton versus Dingley Dell. Dickens wrote it in 1837 when he was in his early twenties. This was four years after John Nyren's book with its 'Full directions for playing the elegant and manly game of cricket' was first published. So even if his first-hand knowledge of the game was limited, Dickens had no excuse for getting the details wrong. However, he set the action in the 1820s, well before Nyren's book appeared.

Dickens, being Dickens, wasn't interested in technical detail but in creating an impression and, in this particular case, in making us laugh. He sets a scene which is instantly recognisable but wouldn't get past the sports editor.

The wickets were pitched, and so were a couple of marquees for the rest and refreshment of the contending parties. The game had not yet commenced. Two or three Dingley Dellers, and All-Muggletonians, were amusing themselves with a majestic air by throwing the ball carelessly from hand to hand; and several other gentlemen dressed like them, in straw hats, flannel jackets, and white trousers – a costume in which they looked very much like amateur stone-masons – were sprinkled about the tents.

I can picture the scene immediately, but what exactly does Dickens mean when he says that the players of both sides were throwing the ball from hand to hand with a majestic air. Was there just the one ball? And, surely, even in those days, the opposing teams wouldn't have thrown the ball to one another, even before play began?

A page or so later play begins.

All-Muggleton had the first innings, and the interest became intense when Mr Dumkins and Mr Podder, two of the most renowned members of that most distinguished club, walked, bat in hand, to their respective wickets. Mr Luffey, the highest ornament of Dingley Dell, was pitched to bowl against the redoubtable Dumkins, and Mr Struggles was selected to do the same kind office for the hitherto unconquered Podder. Several players were stationed to 'look out' in different parts of the field, and each fixed himself into the proper

attitude by placing one hand on each knee, and stoop-
ing very much as if he were 'making a back' for some
beginner at leap-frog. All the regular players do this sort
of thing; indeed it's generally supposed that it is quite
impossible to look out properly in any other position.

I'm slightly concerned about that phrase 'look out' which
I can't find in Nyren. On the other hand Gilbert White,
writing to his nephew from Selborne on August 1786, adds
a PS to his letter in which he writes, 'Little Tom Clement
is visiting at Petersfield, where he plays much at cricket: Tom
bats; his grandmother bowls; and his great-grandmother
watches out!!'

'Watching out', like 'looking out', sounds a rather passive
occupation and not at all what Nyren describes in his section
on fielding which sounds as athletic as it does today. Nor
does Nyren write anything about the curious leap-frog posture
adopted by Dickens's fielders. They sound rather static
compared with Nyren's. Of one position, for example, Nyren
says, 'With the constant movement, therefore in covering his
ground, and closely backing up, the eyes, legs and hands of
the middle wicket are never unoccupied. This situation will
furnish lively employment for an active young gentleman.'

Not many active young gentlemen or constant movement
on the Muggleton ground in *Pickwick Papers*. But that's village
cricket for you. Then as now.

Anyway, we're all ready.

The umpires were stationed behind the wickets; the
scorers were prepared to notch the runs; a breathless
silence ensued. Mr Luffey retired a few paces behind
the wicket of the passive Podder, and applied the ball

to his right eye for several seconds. Dumkins confidently awaited its coming with his eyes fixed on the motions of Luffey.

'Play!' suddenly cried the bowler. The ball flew from his hand straight and swift towards the centre stump of the wicket. The wary Dumkins was on the alert; it fell upon the tip of the bat, and bounded far away over the heads of the scouts, who had just stooped low enough to let it fly over them.

I have no great problem with any of this, surprised though I am to find the bowler rather than the umpire calling out 'Play!' and the fielders being described as 'scouts'. The atmosphere is tangible and persuasive.

Now, however, the great author gives us the whole progress of the match in a single paragraph. It's lovely stuff, but is it cricket?

'Run-run-another. Now, then, throw her up—up with her—stop there—another—no—yes—no—throw her up, throw her up!'—Such were the shouts which followed the stroke, and at the conclusion of which All-Muggleton had scored two. Nor was Podder behindhand in earning laurels wherewith to garnish himself and Muggleton. He blocked the doubtful balls, missed the bad ones, took the good ones, and sent them flying to all parts of the field. The scouts were hot and tired; the bowlers were changed and bowled till their arms ached; but Dumkins and Podder remained unconquered. Did an elderly gentleman essay to stop the progress of the ball, it rolled between his legs or slipped between his fingers. Did a slim gentleman try to catch it, it struck him on the nose, and bounded pleasantly off with redoubled violence, while the slim gentleman's eyes filled with water, and his form writhed with anguish. Was it thrown straight up to the wicket, Dumkins had reached it before the ball. In short, when Dumkins was caught out, and Podder stumped out, All-Muggleton had notched some fifty-four, while the score of the Dingley Dellers was as blank as their faces. The advantage was too great to be recovered. In vain did the eager Luffey, and the enthusiastic Struggles, do all that skill and experience could suggest, to regain the ground Dingley Dell had lost in the contest; —it was of no avail; and in an early period of the winning game Dingley Dell gave in, and allowed the superior prowess of All-Muggleton.

And that's it!

As a piece of writing it's good fun, but as an account of a cricket match it's catastrophic. It looks as if Dumkins and Podder put on fifty-four for the first wicket whereupon the former is out caught and the latter stumped. At this point Dingley Dell's score was nought. Well it would be, wouldn't it? They hadn't even started their innings. Fifty-four doesn't seem a very big score. Admittedly many games were comparatively low scoring, but as long ago as 1777 Hambledon made 403 against All England. If All-Muggleton were on 54 for 2 they would surely have kept batting, especially since the Dingley Dell bowling was wilting badly. And what of the Dingley Dell batting? Dickens tells us nothing about their innings at all. We don't even know whether or not they batted.

The suspicion that Dickens knew nothing about the niceties of the game is confirmed shortly after 'stumps' when Mr

Jingle, already admittedly revealed as a loquacious old poseur, describes a game he once played in the West Indies.

> 'Warm!—red hot—scorching—glowing. Played a match once—single wicket—friend the Colonel—Sir Thomas Blazo—who should get the greatest number of runs.— Won the toss—first innings—seven o'clock A.M.—six natives to look out—went in; kept in—heat intense— natives all fainted—taken away—fresh half-dozen ordered—fainted also—Blazo bowling—supported by two natives—couldn't bowl me out—fainted too— cleared away the Colonel—wouldn't give in—faithful attendant—Quanko Samba—last man left—sun so hot, bat in blisters—ball scorched brown—five hundred and seventy runs—rather exhausted—Quanko mustered up last remaining strength—bowled me out—had a bath, and went out to dinner . . . poor Quanko—never recovered it—bowled on, on my account—bowled off, on his own—died, sir.'

This is clearly a tale of Munchausen implausibility, though no more so in a way than the All-Muggleton–Dingley Dell match. In truth, when it comes to factual accuracy Dickens was better at dinner than at cricket, and his account of the post-match meal at the Blue Lion is a model of precise and barely exaggerated reportage. I particularly like Mr Snodgrass's inebriated and almost indecipherable notes reporting a song supposedly sung by Jingle 'in which the words "bowl", "sparkling", "ruby", "bright" and "wine" are frequently repeated at short intervals'. All of us who have ever been to cricket dinners have heard songs like that, rendered in just such a fashion.

So Dickens was no cricketer, nor even a serious student of the game. On the other hand he obviously very much enjoyed everything that seemed to go with cricket – the food, the drink, the conversation, the bonhomie and perhaps above all the Trevelyanish breaking down of class distinctions which the game seemed to encourage. As his biographer John Forster remarked, Dickens 'confidently looked forward to a time when there would be a more intimate union than exists between the different classes in the state, a union that should embrace alike the highest and the lowest.'

In later years when he was playing the country squire at his grandish house, Gads Hill, near Chatham, he used to stage grand cricket matches at which the landlord of the Falstaff Inn was allowed to have a drinking-booth at the ground. There was never any trouble. On another occasion he put on an athletics meet with foot-races for the villagers. Between two and three thousand people attended.

'Among other oddities,' he reported, 'we had a Hurdle Race for Strangers. One man (he came in second) ran 120 yards and leaped over ten hurdles, in twenty seconds *with a pipe in his mouth and smoking it all the time.* "If it hadn't been for your pipe," I said to him at the winning-post, "you would have been first." "I beg your pardon, sir," he answered, "but if it hadn't been for my pipe, I should have been nowhere."'

This reminded me of Julian Williams of Caerhays Castle, who told me about a demon bowler at his local Cornish club, Gorran, who invariably bowled while smoking a pipe. Was there once a certain sort of British approach to athletic competition in which pipe-smoking played a part? Many of my hearty sporting schoolteachers were inveterate pipe-smokers though never as far as I can recall while actually performing on the playing field. Pipe-smoking while hurdling or playing cricket seems a particularly Dickensian thing to do. J.M. Barrie must have thought so too, because while fielding close to the wicket for his beloved Allahakbarries he was said to be 'sometimes incommoded by his pipe'.

To smoke a pipe or even a cigarette at any level of games playing would be unthinkable today on many different grounds, and yet it would be completely acceptable in the sort of cricket Dickens was writing about. For part of the point of what he was describing was that it was not very good but it didn't much matter. No one scoffed when the elderly Dingley Dellers let the ball slip through their fingers or the slim ones dropped catches and got hit on the nose. If it was worth doing, it was worth doing badly. Perhaps in the end that was what Dickens taught me about cricket that summer in 1956, when England retained the Ashes and Laker took all those wickets. And, also, that even a cricketing ignoramus could write brilliantly about the game provided he entered into the spirit of it.

The second great literary evocation of village cricket occurs as Chapter Seven of the novel *England, their England* by a Winchester-educated Scot called A.G. or 'Archie' Macdonell. It was first published in 1933 and was recently reprinted, with an introduction by Hugo Vickers. Hugo, no cricketer on his own admission, has loved the book since he was about eight and had to declaim some of it from memory. This normally puts people off, but in Hugo's case it caused him to fall in love with it. I thought that although the cricket match is endlessly anthologised, the book of which it is part was barely remembered. Hugo, who regards it as a classic hymn to the values and virtues of Englishness, tells me that this is not the case.

The cricket match in question is played between a team raised by a man called Hodge and a village called Fordenden.

In real life – for this is cricket-*à-clef* – the village is, according to Hugo, a cross between Rodmell in Sussex and Fordcombe in Kent. Eric Midwinter, citing Alec Waugh, also believes Fordenden to be partly based on Fordcombe but makes no mention of Rodmell and instead cites Bridge and Ditchling. Both writers agree that Mr Hodge was Sir John Squire, to whom Macdonell dedicated his book and for whose paper, the *London Mercury*, he contributed acerbic reviews. Squire was a considerable figure in his own day, a legend in his own lunchtime, and even merits an entry in my 1954 edition of the *Concise Oxford Dictionary of English Literature*. I doubt whether he would merit an entry in many reference books nowadays, but he was still alive then and the *Dictionary* says, 'Squire, Sir John Collings, poet, critic and anthologist, recognised as a leader in the immediate post-war period of the "Georgian poets", editor, till recently of the *London Mercury*, famous as a parodist (*Collected Parodies*, 1921) and essayist (*Grub St. Nights*, 1924 &c).'

Jeremy Paul, the scriptwriter and passionate cricketer, has written a sprightly history of the club that Squire founded and for which Paul played. In it he reveals that Alec Waugh, Evelyn's brother who features in the fictional match as Bobby Southcott, wrote that Squire was no cricketer, knew that he was no cricketer and knew that the Invalids knew it too. But there was a conspiracy of silence on the matter.

The first game seems to have been played at West Wycombe in 1919 or 1920 and was between a team of authors captained by Squire and the local side which included Squire's uncle by marriage, E.W. Hornung, creator of Raffles, brother-in-law of Sir Arthur Conan Doyle. (Doyle was a better cricketer than most writers. Good enough to make a century once for MCC against Scotland.) Hornung bowled Squire for a duck that day, but even so Squire resolved that 'his' side would live to play another day. He changed the name from the Old Age Pensioners to the Invalids, declared that the colours should be hospital blue and old gold, which were the colours of wartime officers' pyjamas, and that the club's badge should be a pair of crossed crutches.

Macdonell's match was played one sunny Saturday and our hero, Donald, a young Scot modelled on Macdonell himself, joins his team-mates at the Embankment entrance to Charing Cross station, whence they set off by charabanc to the countryside, arriving, via various pubs, three hours late at the village of Fordenden.

This is Donald's first sight of rural England and Macdonell describes the scene in two long paragraphs of magic lyricism. Of the centre stage, for instance, he writes: 'The cricket field itself was a mass of daisies and buttercups and dandelions, tall grasses and purple vetches and thistle-down, and great clumps of dark-red sorrel, except, of course, for the oblong patch in the centre – mown, rolled, watered – a smooth, shining emerald of grass, the Pride of Fordenden, the Wicket.'

Apart from all the traditional vegetation of the traditional English country village Fordenden also has a pub called the Three Horseshoes, a church, a vicar, a blacksmith, and elderly gaffers on a bench with tankards. 'The entire scene,' writes Macdonell, 'was perfect to the last detail.'

The setting may have been perfect but the condition of the visiting team was far from ideal. When play started they were still two men short and, with the possible exception of young Donald, they were at least slightly the worse for drink. There's a distinctly dodgy moment earlier when Donald, almost inebriated by the beauty of the English village, turns to gaze at the Three Horseshoes, thinks that the men with the pints of beer outside it are vaguely familiar and realises with a jolt that they are his team-mates. This sort of thing may happen less often nowadays, but I have come across one such club which always batted first on the grounds that they would never have a complete fielding side when play began and that the lower half of the batting line-up must have an hour or two in which to sober up or sleep off lunch.

Just as the the *England, their England* players are about to start, two men short, at Fordenden, a motor-car arrives with the two missing players and one other, who assures everyone that he had a firm invitation from Mr Hodge and was determined to play. Hurried rearrangements were made between the two skippers and, instead of nine-a-side, they agreed to play twelve-a-side. (A certain leeway in regulations seems to me to be an essential part of true village cricket. It is essential that to an extent and within reason the two captains should be able to vary procedures to suit local conditions.)

Mr Hodge wins the toss, chooses to bat and sends out his openers, a sound club cricketer called James Livingstone and an eighteen-stone former Cambridge blue called Boone. Boone turns out to be an execrable cricketer and it transpires, belatedly, that his blue was for rowing and not cricket as Mr Hodge thought.

Fordenden are captained by the local baker, just as modern day Boconnoc are captained by the baker from Liskeard who also does the team teas. The opening bowler, very fast and very erratic, is the village blacksmith, a figure who these days, of course, seldom survives. He bowls the club cricketer with the fourth ball of his first over, having already conceded four byes and a six. Within no time at all the visitors have struggled to 10 for 3 with one man retired hurt.

It is already apparent, even at this early stage, that Macdonell understands cricket a great deal better than Dickens. He is also

terrific at thumbnail character sketches in which his characters' cricketing skills – or lack of them – complement the
personal quirks and qualities they display in what a non-cricketing fanatic would describe as 'real life'. The thunderous but
erratic fast bowling of the blacksmith echoes the man's burly
and splenetic nature; so does the slow left-hand bowling of the
local rate-collector 'whose whole life was one of infinite patience
and guile'. This man obviously bowled as he lived – or lived
as he bowled, depending on one's view of cricket and life.

The next man in is 'the famous novelist Robert Southcott
himself'.

I confess to an advantage here because I glimpsed Alec
Waugh, the real-life character on whom Mr Southcott is
based, admittedly in much later life, and although I never
saw him play cricket I feel that Macdonell has him to a T.
He was by the time I encountered him a very small but still
elegant figure given to brocade waistcoats and annual visits
to England from his Caribbean home. These were timed to
coincide with the Lord's Test match and the annual dinner
of the Sherborne School Old Boys' Society, from which he
had been expelled years earlier for writing his allegedly scur-
rilous novel based on school life.

Just as this celebrity, holding his bat as delicately as if it
was a flute or fan, was picking his way through the daisies
and thistle-down towards the wicket, Mr Hodge rushed
anxiously, tankard in hand, from the Three Horseshoes
and bellowed in a most unpoetical voice: 'Play carefully,
Bobby. Keep your end up. Runs don't matter.'

'Very well, Bill,' replied Mr Southcott sedately. Donald
was interested by this little exchange. It was Team Spirit
at work – the captain instructing his man to play a type

of game that was demanded by the state of the team's fortunes, and the individual loyally suppressing his instincts to play a different type of game.

Mr Southcott took guard modestly, glanced furtively round the field as if it was an impertinence to suggest that he would survive long enough to make a study of the fieldsmen's positions worth while, and hit the rate-collector's first ball over the Three Horseshoes into a hayfield.

And so on, the famous novelist carts the rate-collector and his team-mates all over the place until as the score teeters towards respectability and he himself has made a cavalier fifty. At this point Mr Hodge emerges once more from the pub and shouts out, 'You needn't play safe any more, Bob. Play your own game.' Whereupon Mr Southcott falls into a kind of 'cricketing trance' and scores only one run in the next quarter of an hour before being given out by an elderly and partisan umpire.

The only other interesting moment is when a young American called Shakespeare Pollock comes to the crease and behaves as if he were playing baseball, bunts the ball towards square leg, throws down his bat and hurtles towards cover. This signals a collapse and the whole side is out without further addition.

This looks like a winning score when the visitors' answer to the blacksmith, Major Hawker clean bowls six Fordenden men and breaks a stump. At the end of this spell the village is 11 for 6 and the Major vanishes. He vanishes, of course, to the pub where, when his team-mates find him, he has already consumed a quart and a half of mild and bitter. Dragged back to the pitch, he proceeds to bowl nothing more alarming than slow full-tosses which the rate collector and the baker hit all over the place, and the score mounts steadily until, after some felicitous run-outs and stumpings, the sides are absolutely level with the last Fordenden pair at the wicket. This means the blacksmith, of course, who is limping heavily after being no-balled by Mr Harcourt and is in a stupendous rage. He hits the first ball miles high and pandemonium ensues with mass collisions and a catch by the American off two heads and the wicketkeeper's bottom.

Both teams then adjourn to the Three Horseshoes, where they spend the evening. Mr Harcourt makes a speech in Italian about the glories of England and Donald gets home to Chelsea at one in the morning.

Sadly the men on whom the members of this eccentric team are modelled, that is Squire's Invalids, are not now much remembered. Apart from the Hodge/Squire figure, Donald/Macdonell and Southcott/Waugh, they are mostly writers, famous in their own day but no longer, alas, in ours.

Apart from the characters already identified, Mr Harcourt, the demon umpire who unhinged the demon blacksmith by no-balling him, was J.B. Morton, a brilliantly comic columnist for the *Daily Express*; Major Hawker was R.B. Lowe, aka a sometime MP called Reginald Berkeley who wrote *The Lady with the Lamp*, which in 1951 became a movie of the same name with Anna Neagle as Florence Nightingale; and the fat wicketkeeper was a publisher called Cecil Palmer. One or two serious cricketers occasionally turned out, including the great Australian wicketkeeper, W.A. Oldfield, and the Surrey captain, P.G.H. (Percy) Fender, whose daughter sometimes came too. A.P. Herbert is also supposed to have played; likewise G.K. Chesterton and Hilaire Belloc, though they sound more like spectators than participants. Chesterton is still remembered in the club history for the telegram he once sent his wife, presumably attempting to find the setting for an Invalid match: 'Am in Market Harborough, where should I be?'

Squire's attitude to the team was fanatical but realistic. 'You can ask,' he wrote, 'the most unlikely, the most aged, decrepit and unpractised of men to play for a scratch team and you will find they are invariably willing . . . if a man won't play for any other reason he will play for the sake of a pleasant excursion or because of the exceptional opportunity of raising a thirst.'

Such an attitude and certainly its expression would be incorrect if not actionable in the prim early years of the twenty-first century, though something similar, in my experience, lingers on.

The third in the pantheon of great village matches in literature is Hugh de Selincourt's novel *The Cricket Match*. John Arlott thought it the best of all cricket novels, and John Bright-Holmes, a cricket anthologist of an erudition which almost matches that of Prof. Midwinter, says it is 'probably still the best single novel written about cricket in general and village cricket in particular'. It has to be said – as Prof. Midwinter suggests in his exhaustive study of the matter – that the competition is not exactly stiff, but the fact remains that many people regard this book as a classic. Indeed Midwinter himself claims that although in his study 'the lens will swing from Charles Dickens and Jane Austen to James Joyce and Iris Murdoch, Hugh de Selincourt, given his masterpiece, *The Cricket Match*, has no need to be embarassed by the company he is invited to keep.'

Well, up to a point.

De Selincourt was at school at Dulwich, which also

educated two contemporary masters of English prose in P.G.
Wodehouse (three years junior to de Selincourt) and
Raymond Chandler. Wodehouse was keen enough on cricket
to name his best-known character after a Warwickshire slow
bowler called Jeeves and himself once took 7 for 50 bowling fast for his school against Tonbridge. Chandler is not
someone you'd immediately associate with the game.

De Selincourt reviewed books and plays for a number of
London publications and also wrote a collection of cricket
short stories and a book called *The Saturday Match*, but it is
for *The Cricket Match* that he is best remembered. The novel
tells the story of a single match between the fictitious teams
of Tillingfold and Raveley. For seven years de Selincourt
captained the Sussex village of Storrington, and it is generally accepted that Tillingfold is Storrington in thin disguise
and that the fictional home captain, Paul Gauvinier, is de
Selincourt in equally thin, if rather glamourised disguise.

Wisden in its obituary said, in a rather toffee-nosed dismissal,
that there was no evidence that de Selincourt was 'a specially
accomplished player himself'. Yet in his novel he or his character wins the match with a brilliant last over which opens
with his fastest ball, is followed by a slow yorker, and then
a couple of nice good-length leg-breaks, the second of which
induces the match-winning catch. I somehow doubt whether
the real-life de Selincourt would have been capable of such
felicitous bowling control. It doesn't matter. It's a novel, after
all, and why shouldn't an author indulge in a little fanciful
wish-fulfilment? However, I don't think I very much care
for Gauvinier. He sounds rather a prig. I would prefer to
have played for Mr Hodge, drunk and crotchety though he
might have been. And even though Macdonell's account in
England, their England wasn't published until 1933, Squire's

Invalids must have been rollicking around the south of England, including de Selincourt's part of West Sussex, at much the same period in the twenties.

Another niggle I have about this classic book is that although de Selincourt is adamant about it being a 'village' I'm not at all sure it would satisfy the rigorous demands of Ben and Tim Brocklehurst and their colleagues who organise the National Village Cricket Championship. Yes, the author calls it a village; yes, there is a mill-pond; yes, the railway line is five miles away; yes, there are 'picturesque cottages' from which emanate early morning smoke; yes, church; yes, vicarage.

But what of this: 'There are two general stores and one London emporium, three butchers, four bakers, three cobblers, a barber, three builders; a bank, a dissenting chapel, two cycle shops, three tea shops, a garage and seven public houses.' A London emporium and seven pubs in a village? Come on. Tillingfold is no more a village in the accepted sense than the ancient town of Usk! Why, there is one house nearby on which the owners have lavished £80,000. Eighty thousand pounds in 1921! What sort of place is this?

Perhaps I am nit-picking. After all, if the author says a place is a village, then village it is. And the cricket being played on that August day in 1921 is recognisably that quirky and elusive game called 'village cricket' and everything is a jolly good show, full of such desirable matters as a last-wicket stand between the fifty-year-old club secretary, whose wife is concerned that he is over-exerting himself, and the fifteen-year-old schoolboy, whose mother looks 'simply ripping'. At the end of one over the old chap comes over to the 'young whippersnapper' and says, 'You're playing beautifully, boy, a lovely nice game, boy.' (The author remarks, 'The boy was fifteen and the man was fifty, but neither felt the least incongruity in their ages; they were just sportsmen on equal terms.')

Many such disparities are evidenced on the field of play, and even G.M.Trevelyan would have felt vindicated at seeing how cricket made them all equal – young and old, rich and poor, aristocratic and common, clever and downright stupid. At the day's end when Tillingfold have, thanks to skipper Gauvinier, triumphed by just two runs, de Selincourt pictures the community as it celebrates quietly. Up at the big house young Edgar Trine is smoking a cigar with his father and two visitors while the ladies have retired; Dick Fanshawe has bicycled round to his old friend Gauvinier to discuss the game 'with life and art and morals thrown in, of course'. And, finally, 'The band stopped playing and dispersed, the gossiping groups broke up and straggled away, some singing uproarious catches along the still lanes. Slowly the square emptied, the colour went out of the sky, and night descended peacefully upon the village of Tillingfold. Rich and poor, old and young, were seeking sleep.'

And meanwhile I doubt very much whether the chara-banc conveying Sir John Squire aka Mr Hodge and his team of inebriates has even yet made it to the Charing Cross embankment.

Perhaps it is because I encountered the Dickens and the Macdonell as a child that I so cherish them. Perhaps it is because I came late to *The Cricket Match* that I find its charms so resistible.

I have been re-reading Benny Green's 1979 introduction to the book and wondering where I go wrong. Green's principal passions were jazz and cricket, though he was something of a polymath with an agreeable enthusiasm for many things. He was also, importantly, a Jewish boy from the East

End of London and a living rebuke, I believe, to those who think that a love of cricket, and perhaps especially of village cricket, is a class thing, confined to toffs with funny accents and private educations. It isn't – sport and games transcend all social divisions, which isn't to say that they don't also contain social and sexual anomalies and attract the affection and even fanatacism of people we don't much like for all sorts of reasons including class.

Benny Green thought *The Cricket Match* has 'gradually ascended to the status of a minor classic'. Barrie wrote that it was 'the best story about cricket or any other game'. I have to say that I think it's worn less than well and has dated more than the game it portrays.

Nevertheless de Selincourt was convinced that 'cricket was the greatest game and village cricket its most profound expression. He even went so far as believing that village cricket 'takes off from cricket to the even greater game of living, and that something is the spirit of active good-will, the finest and most precious thing in life'. I sense that Dickens and Macdonell might have believed much the same but that, like many of us, they would have flinched from actually saying so.

There have been other literary evocations of village cricket before and since. Gideon Haigh's recent account of a season playing with his Melbourne parks side, *The Vincibles*, demonstrates that something surprisingly similar (hard-fought, often incompetent, ubiquitously nicknamed and so on) exists down-under. Jeremy Paul's *Sing Willow* about the Invalids and Vernon Coleman's *The Village Cricket Tour* are recent literary reminders that the traditional form and spirit of the game are alive and well.

I also particularly commend Mary Russell Mitford who, in 1832, argued that there was nothing 'more animating or delightful than a cricket match', and the incomparable J.L. Carr, who in an elegiac and characteristically miniature volume called *The First Saturday in May*, after a day of Shropshire cricket and missed trains in 1936 was 'left remembering the heat of the day, the burden of fielding ankle-deep in Bridgnorth's cattle-mart, snow storms of hillside blossom. And wondering if a change of trains, or for that matter, a change of anything, really is for the better.'

A love of village cricket implies just such a Carr-like affection for a traditional England and mistrust of change. In acknowledgement of both these traits I stick to my belief that literature has been paramount in defining my understanding of village cricket and that much as I have enjoyed and admired a number of literary village cricket matches just three stand out above the rest. All Muggleton versus Dingley Dell; Mr Hodge's XI versus Fordenden, and Tillingfold versus Raveley.

With a little reluctance I'm happy to end these reflections with Benny Green's verdict that 'So far as the Tillingfold-Raveley match is concerned, it passed long ago into that mythology which knows no ending.'

On second thoughts, no I'm not.

I'm going to end with a thought from perhaps the greatest of all contemporary cricket-loving writers: Harold Pinter. What's more, I'm going to keep it pure and simple and as enigmatic and question-raising yet alarmingly certain and untentative as a Pinter line almost invariably is.

I wrote to him, as I promised in my proposal, to see what he thought the best of all village cricket grounds.

The reply came back on a postcard.

It said:

'Great Hampden – by miles. Harold.'

4

Centuries of Cornish Cream

I have ranged far and wide geographically and socio-economically, but another unexpected spanner entered the works half-way through my researches – a spanner which I found on the one hand immensely enhancing but on the other unexpectedly diminishing.

Television.

Every schoolboy knows that TV has had a quantum effect on our appreciation and understanding of cricket as of almost anything else in life. The instant replay, the immediate close-up, the ability to demonstrate without a scintilla of doubt that a ball would or would not have hit the wicket have all made the position of umpire virtually impossible. Millions of viewers sitting in their armchairs at home have a more accurate impression of crucial moments than the man in the white coat at the wicket. Those same armchair viewers would, in an earlier age, have relied on the crackling radio or the purple pen for their cricketing information. But what is the point of *Test Match Special* or Neville Cardus now that we have 'Hawkeye' and Channel Four?

Of course there is no substitute for the smell of mown grass, the buzz of a crowd in conversation, warm beer and wasps in the sandwiches, but you know more about the details in the middle of the pitch if you stay at home. I love those ill-informed conversations in the Tavern Stand at Lord's. In the summer of 2003 I sat there watching England demolish South Africa from a position somewhere over the square-leg boundary.

'I didn't hear a snick.'

'That didn't carry.'

'Stumped!'

'No, he played on.'

'Can't see that there's much in this wicket for the off-spinner.'

'He'll have a much better chance going over the wicket.'

'Oh come on, umpire, where's your white stick!'

Truth was, we couldn't see a thing.

The television effect on this book was more personal and more immediate.

I was getting on with my researches much as suggested in my original proposal and outline, though with deviations dictated by circumstance such as not being able to write about the modern Martock club, when I received an invitation to attend a gathering in Polperro just down the Cornish coast from Fowey where I live. A couple of local TV producers had decided to gather up as many writers living in the area as possible and see if together they couldn't develop some initatives and take advantage of some of the European money sloshing around in poverty-stricken, under-developed Cornwall.

Our host was David Taylor, who had an impressive list of credentials stretching back through *Panorama* and *World in Action*, radio's *File on Four*, and much else besides. He had worked as a reporter on the *Newcastle Journal* and the *Manchester Guardian*. He had been the Executive Producer of the *Great Railway Journeys of the World* but, most important, he was passionate about cricket. As a schoolboy he had evidently captained his Grammar School team in Newcastle and gone on, if I understood right, to open for London University and even have a trial for Middlesex, and might have gone on to higher things were it not for a freak ball which broke a bone in his cheek. An aside: the thing about cricketer's bullshit is that when it is delivered with authority by a man of a certain age with eyes and knees which now make it impossible for him to prove his cricketing ability one way or another, you don't really have any alternative but to nod submissively and take it all at face value – he might have been a veritable Len Hutton or he might just as well have been absolute rubbish. But David was palpably genuine, and what was certain was that he was incredibly keen. And when I said that I was writing a book about village cricket his eyes started to revolve in a way in which they did not revolve when rival writers were telling him about martyred Celtic saints, eighteenth-century pasty-making, or the influence of the Camborne School of Mines on the Bolivian tin industry.

'I think there might be a TV series in that,' he said, after a while.

And in due course there was. I have no idea what alchemist's skills David used to persuade the powers that be at Carlton TV to commission a series on 'Village Cricket', but he did. At first the series was to be four half-hour episodes. Then, mysteriously, the four expanded into six. Wonderful!

My last major TV experience was in the early eighties when Thames TV filmed some of my whodunits. On the whole it was an enjoyable episode, but two thoughts in particular stuck in my mind. The first was that I assumed that TV was a 'licence to print money', as the late Lord Thomson of Fleet said so memorably of his ownership of Scottish TV in the sixties. Er, no. The money I got paid for the rights was gratefully received but not the stuff of which retirement to the South of France is made, and when my books were reissued in paperback I was told that the televised versions of them had been so unsuccessful that they 'damaged the sale of the books'.

Even more important was the notion that a writer could ever enjoy more than the slightest control over the television version of his work. With the television of my crime books the production team and script writers were charm personified but changes were continual. I was fairly certain that something similar would happen with the TV series on village cricket, and so, in a manner of speaking, it turned out.

The first confusion occurred with Boconnoc. Boconnoc, a great house and estate just south and east of Lostwithiel, was in some respects the inspiration for my quest and for this book.

They have played cricket at Boconnoc continually since 1846. The ground, set in the Fortescue family's deer park, is achingly beautiful. The place itself – though not, sadly, the cricket – is first mentioned in the Domesday Survey of 1086 when it is recorded that 'Osferth holds from Count Mortain Bochenod. He also held it before 1066 and paid tax for 1 virgate [30 acres], half a hide there however [60 acres], land for 8 ploughs; 1 plough there with slave, 2 villagers and 6 small holders. Woodland 100 acres, pasture 40 acres. Formerly 40s, value now 15s. 15 goats.'

Andrew Foot, for many years an English teacher at the Royal Russell School in Surrey (most famous former pupil the actor Martin Clunes), once captain of the cricket club, subsequently umpire, has a house on the estate and is an expert on its history.

'There is no clue about how long the estate had existed before 1066,' he says, 'but for it to be so well established by then, it must have been many years.'

Around a hundred of us sat down the night I was the guest speaker at the annual club dinner mentioned at the beginning – a roast turkey meal at the Westberry Hotel in Bodmin. The president was a Dorset-born and -accented farmer called John Foot, who had retired as a player but still umpired. It was John who had approached me on learning that I was living locally and had published books on cricket. The diners that evening ranged from teenagers to pensioners. It's one of the many attractive features of cricket at the grass roots. The game is not only supported and followed by the very young and the very old but also played by different generations, often in the same teams. That night in Bodmin the youngest present were enthusiastic twelve-year-olds and the oldest had once been coached by Denis Compton's brother Leslie.

After dinner I told stories about Denis Compton and Brian Johnston and people asked questions about what they were 'really' like, and then my wife presented the cups and trophies. The young star batsman seemed to walk off with more than his fair share, but there was one for the best Second Eleven batsman, bowler and fielder and another for the person who had contributed most to the club – who turned out to be the groundsman. The sandwich and tea makers got a special round of applause, and there were flowers for the elderly woman in the wheelchair who had served the club all her life and was fighting cancer. Afterwards my wife drew the raffle.

Everything seemed just as it should be – gloriously unchanging. And yet this wasn't just some quaint time-warped cameo set in aspic. The farmers, and there were several, were battling against everything from rapacious supermarkets to the ban on beef-on-the-bone. They were working so hard they could barely get time off for cricket. There was much muttering because the star batsman had defected to another club who were paying him 'appearance money'. Here, in Cornwall East, Division Three. The leagues and profession-alism are everywhere.

This was England all right (though the Cornish don't like to be described as 'English'): traditional England on one hand, but very modern England on another. Above all, I thought, an England which simply doesn't get reported in the modern media and which most city dwellers neither know nor under-stand.

I first saw cricket at Boconnoc in the early summer of 1996 shortly after moving to Cornwall. There had been an open day in aid of charity, and the grounds of the great house were a riot of azaleas, camellias, rhododendrons and I know not what. The house was empty, propped up by a giant crutch of a wooden flying buttress, and we wandered round peering through windows; contemplated the view to the silted lake across a valley of surprising width and softness for such a supposedly craggy peninsular county; and I thought of Walter de la Mare and the traveller knocking on the moonlit door. '"Tell them I came, and no one answered, / That I kept my word," he said.' Despite the crowds the place felt sad, neglected, possibly even haunted.

Then, driving away through the sylvan, undulating park dappled with deer I saw in the distance that most English of English sights: men in white, flickering to and fro on an oval of mown grass. I stopped the car, reflecting momentarily that, of course, despite its apparent Englishness this was a Cornish scene and therefore actually Celtic and un-English. Which prompted questions on the nature of Englishness and of cricket which I only half-formulated because I was so utterly seduced by the beauty of the scene.

I was far enough away from play to be deceived into thinking that the flannelled fools themselves were all lissome athletes if not actually Greek Gods with the looks and abilities of a latter-day C.B. Fry. I knew, of course, that this was ridiculous. This was village cricket. The players were bound to come in all shapes and sizes and they would not be very good at cricket. No matter. Not even 'no matter'; it's half the point.

I didn't want to get too close, perhaps because I didn't want my illusions destroyed. A small boy was bowling. He reminded me of my prep school self, shuffling in rather clumsily, left arm up very high, eyeing the batsman with his crooked elbow as the rifle sight, turning his right arm stiff and slow, releasing the ball as the arm started its descent and watching as the cherry-red orb rose in a high almost donkey-drop arc before pitching just about on the wicket, not far off a length and not unduly wide of the off stump.

The batsman could have been the boy's father, having, I realised on closer scrutiny, the bulk of middle age and a fancy cap, hooped and old-fashioned. Leaning forward into a tolerable imitation of the forward defensive shot demonstrated by D.R. Jardine in my school English prize copy of *The Lonsdale Book of Cricket*.

The leather and the willow produced the satisfactory noise that they always do when they collide in the middle of the bat, and the ball rolled slowly back down the pitch. The little boy, only a few yards from the batsman who might have been his father, picked it up, rubbed it up and down on his white-flannelled bottom and walked back to start the whole performance all over again.

It was very quiet. The sun shone. Fielders bent and unbent and one or two chewed blades of grass. The small boy bowled again and his proto-father played the same respectful defensive shot. There were one or two spectators in deck-chairs; others lay on their stomachs half asleep. Deer glanced up from beyond the outfield but did not, as they sometimes do, stop play. Presently there would be tea and sandwiches prepared by wives and mothers. I watched until the end of the over. Nothing untoward took place.

On another day in another year it was bitter cold in the deer park and Boconnoc were struggling against St Minver. 'They've got a Pakistani, St Minver,' said a frozen spectator, hugging himself against the cold. 'Not a real Pakistani, mind. He comes from London.' And sure enough there was a trim dark spin bowler wheeling away in a manner which looked a notch or two above the lowly level of the average player in this competition. And sure enough St Minver won and at the end of the season were promoted. Boconnoc lost and stayed where they were. In a perverse way I was rather pleased.

On both occasions it was very quiet and peaceful and much, I later learned, as it had been for a hundred and fifty years since the present owner's great-grandfather wrote in his diary for 1846, 'Cricket Club established and first meeting held in the park.'

In the nineteenth century teams had put up at the Talbot in Lostwithiel. This is the same pub, incidentally, where, at a meeting in 1895, the idea of a Cornish county cricket club was first proposed. Lostwithiel, although the nearest town to Boconnoc, was still an hour by horse and cart – then the preferred mode of transport for most visitors. Bodmin, some ten miles away, once seemed very distant, but the modern club draws its players from a much wider area than in the early days, and Bodmin is as near the residential hub as Bocconoc itself. Until 1914 at least there were droves of workers in the fields and on the estate, and cricket was one of their principal sources of entertainment. Today Boconnoc's players are as likely to be bank managers or estate agents as farm labourers or estate workers. And they come from relatively far and wide.

Boconnoc is a beautiful and historic cricket ground in a beautiful and historic place. Because it was also in a sense the inspiration for this book, and so it had to be included. For similar reasons it seemed only sensible to include it in the TV series, and David and his ex-BBC associate and wife Laura agreed in principle. When I took them along to see Anthony Fortescue, who runs the estate on behalf of his father Desmond and who is president of the cricket club, they became even keener. We had an agreeable and constructive chat in the estate office, during which I formally challenged Anthony to a match, to be televised, between my team and one of his own choosing and Anthony, while professing relative incompetence as a practising cricketer, cheerfully agreed. Afterwards Anthony showed us round the ancestral home in order to demonstrate the extraordinary process of renovation. David and Laura were duly impressed, to such an extent that they even wanted to make a separate programme about what the Fortescues were doing to their house. Everyone parted on the best of terms, Anthony confiding to me in private that he was more than suitably impressed by the television makers' provenance, charm and obvious abilities.

All completely splendid. David told me that he and Laura were to have lunch with Anthony and his wife Elizabeth. He also described in affectionate detail an evening with the club in the newly licensed pavilion, where drink was taken, more pleasantries exchanged, everyone was on first-name terms and everything was the acme of bonhomie and mutual back-slapping.

And then suddenly the club official who had been on such breezy first-name terms with David at the evening meeting wrote a formal 'Dear Mr Taylor' letter saying that the club wished to have nothing further to do with any TV project of any kind. And Anthony continued to be perfectly nice to me, but the subject of my televised cricket match was resolutely evaded. He even asked me to play for his team in the annual president's match against the club – I would be away and so declined on grounds of availability – and encouraged me to bring a team to play against some visiting barristers and Eton Ramblers from 'up-country'. But TV was off.

This in no way diminishes my fondness for Boconnoc. It remains as beautiful a ground as you will find anywhere. The Fortescues' involvement gives it a slightly quaint, feudal quality which has become comparatively rare though it was once almost the norm. The cricket is, well, ordinary. At the time of writing they have just lost to Veryan, a pretty village on the fashionable Roseland peninsula. They are fifth from bottom of the county's Division Three East, which is currently propped up by their neighbours at Lanhydrock – another great house once belonging to the Robartes but now in the hands of the National Trust. The leaders are my home team of Fowey, where I am a vice-president. Fowey celebrated their thirtieth anniversary with a jolly lunch the other day. Thirtieth anniversary of their re-foundation, for the club was originally founded in 1856, only to die out in the sixties. Fowey, of course, is an ancient and historic town, not a village, but that's another story. Meanwhile I think fifth from bottom of Division Three is probably just about right for Boconnoc.

The Cornish were playing 'grass-root' if not precisely 'village' cricket long before the Fortescues started up at Boconnoc. If you need proof then you can find it in as near a permanent form as you could imagine. One of the many good things about Cornwall is that they seem to rather like writers and if they want something unveiled, for example, they are almost as likely to ask a writer (one to unveil something) as they are to ask someone like a Lord Lieutenant or even the Duke. One day Michael Williams, publisher, writer and founder of the Cornish Crusaders, a wandering club which would, I think, be mildly affronted to be described as playing 'village cricket' but which nonetheless maintains many of the traditions and values which I associate with the concept, asked me to unveil a plaque.

My plaque was a fine gilded slate on the wall of the White Hart Inn at St Teath, a mid-Cornwall village named after St Tetha, one of the twenty-four children of King Brecon of Wales. Tetha (was she really called that, or was she christened by a priest with a lisp?) had a number of saintly siblings including Mabyn and Endellion, but the village's true claim to fame is now commemorated by the slate on the wall of the pub. The inscription reads: 'First Cricket in Cornwall. 3rd July 1781. Single wicket championship at the back of the White Hart, St Teath. Gentlemen Farmers competing and a handsome silver laced hat for the champion.'

At the moment no one knows who did the 'hat-trick' nor exactly who the contestants were. Such information as we have was culled from the pages of the *Sherborne Mercury* which, according to the local historian, Ian Clarke, was once the main newspaper for the whole of the south-west of Britain. It was Clarke, now studying for a Ph.D. in the social history of cricket at de Montfort University in Leicester, who unearthed this arcane piece of the Celtic past.

When I consulted Stephen Green, the almost impossibly erudite librarian and archivist at Lord's, he could find no earlier reference to Cornish cricket than 1813, the year of the foundation of the county club. I can't help wondering if this had something to do with the fact that the St Teath contest for the hat pre-dates the founding of MCC by a full six years. In other words they were playing cricket in Cornwall well before it came to St John's Wood, and the White Hart can now plausibly pull rank on the Tavern at Lord's. The committee won't like that.

We were lucky with the weather on the day of the unveiling – not that rain would have stopped our play. Michael Williams local resident, had organised the occasion and procured the slate from the world-famous Delabole quarry just down the road. Julian Williams (no relation), the County Vice Lord Lieutenant and President of the Cornwall County Cricket Club came over from his home at Caerhays Castle, and Canon Ken Rogers, the former Rector of Bodmin with a voice like John Arlott's and another stalwart of Cornish cricket dropped by on his way to preach at Tewkesbury Abbey.

The star, however, was the Bishop of Truro, the Right Revd William Ind. Bishop Bill is passionate about his cricket and was due to turn out two days later for the Crusaders against Truro School. In the course of his homily in front of the unveiled slate, he admitted that the previous weekend in the cathedral his mind had wandered occasionally 'from The Lord's business to the business at Lord's'. He had even put down a modest prayer on behalf of the England team and was pleased that it seemed to have been answered. He would like the fact to be known.

The bishop's hero, on whose style his own spin bowling is allegedly based, is Doug Wright, once of Kent and England, but not only is he, I guess, the only bishop now playing, he has the sort of encyclopaedic knowledge of the game that can recite whole chunks of *Wisden* the way other people once declaimed Shakespeare. I've heard him reel off the entire 1950 Cambridge University team complete with initials. Hugely reassuring. I thought that the ecclesiastical tradition epitomised by Prebendary Wickham of Martock had died out with the retirement of the Revd Andrew Wingfield Digby.

There was something Wodehouseishly timeless about the unveiling of the slate and it was not just the presence of Bishop Bill that made me think that some verities really *are* eternal.

A few days earlier I had been at Lord's for an epic Test match between England and the West Indies. Walsh and Ambrose versus Atherton. The world's most famous cricket ground seemed an extraordinary oasis in a London landscape which can seem increasingly squalid – Londoners themselves seem not to notice the blemishes and disfigurements of what should be one of the world's greatest cities. For those few intoxicating days at Lord's, however, cricket seemed to exert a peculiarly civilising influence. I have seldom sat in a crowd which was so enthralled, partisan and yet so generous. What a breathless hush! What cricket, lovely cricket.

In a quieter, remoter, more rural way, cricket seemed to exercise a similar spell when we commemorated the cattle fair contest in St Teath all those years ago. It was reassuring to see such straight bats being played on the national stage and then a few days later on the village green. Much has happened to spoil the game, but despite everything it is still something to celebrate and I'm very proud to have unveiled a Delabole slate on the wall of a Cornish pub to help in doing so.

After the episcopal blessing we all adjourned to the pool room for a pasty-based lunch provided by the landlord, Barry Burton, who was celebrating his fiftieth year at the pub, having arrived from Nottingham with his parents when he was four. An exile from Sheffield showed me her Bramall Lane autograph book from 1937 (oh my Sutcliffe and my Verity long ago, long ago) and the sports editor of Radio Cornwall conducted interviews in the car park. Bob Flower, who runs cricket, and much of North Cornish life by the sound of it, from Tintagel, recommended his web site (Tintagelweb.co.uk) and we reflected that 1781 was only six years after the introduction of the third stump. (Should it be taken away again, at least when England are batting? Is it time for a fourth or even fifth when Australia are in?)

In 1781 cricket was an emerging force still rivalled by such games as the now forgotten 'gingling' and Sheffield Bowls, condemned by one source as 'unmanly in the extreme'. Those eighteenth-century cattle farmers were real pioneers and without men like them cricket would never have become 'the best-loved game'.

Much of that early game was played between teams, though not always of eleven men. Single-wicket matches, however, were a popular variation. In his seminal book, *The Young Cricketer's Tutor*, published in 1833, John Nyren, one of Hambledon's finest, has a complete section on 'Single Wicket'.

> The parties in a match at single wicket vary in number from one to six on a side. The distance between the wickets is twenty-two yards. At the bowler's wicket, two stumps are placed with a bail upon them; and this the striker, when running, must come to, and strike off, and return to his own wicket. This is counted one run. If the bail should be off, the batter must strike the stump out of the ground. When the party consists of fewer than four on each side, if the striker leave his ground to hit the ball, he will not be permitted to reckon a notch.

And there are those who believe that the great game of cricket has continued unchanged over the centuries!

One of the most famous single-wicket games was in

1810 when Squire Osbaldeston and William Lambert challenged the Revd Lord Frederick Beauclerk (even more eccentric cleric than probendary Wickham) and Mr Howard to a game at Lord's. On the day Osbaldeston was too ill to play but the others refused to postpone the match and Lambert, who thought nothing of walking twenty-five miles to London simply to practise, had to take on Beauclerk and Howard single-handed. In the event he scored 56 and 24 and got the others out for 24 and 42. Osbaldeston's mother watched the match from her carriage and afterwards rewarded the victor with a paper parcel. No one knows what it contained, though speculation suggests bank notes or a gold watch. Certainly not a 'silver laced hat'.

E. V. Lucas, author of *The Hambledon Men*, was a keen advocate of the single-wicket game. He himself used to play for J.M. Barrie's team, the Allahakbarries, though it was said of him that he was 'more at ease in the pavilion than at the crease'. Even in 1906 he was lamenting the demise of single-wicket stuff.

'I wonder,' he wrote, 'if we are ever to see single-wicket matches again. They seem to have gone for ever, with the tall hat, and the grey flannel shirt, and the leg hit; and yet there must in the old days have been as much fun and excitement at a two-hours' single-wicket match as ever is extracted from a three-day county contest.'

As if in a belated answer to this lament Michael Williams himself arranged a single-wicket tournament on behalf of his beloved Cornish Crusaders, to be played one August Sunday in 2003 at Grampound Road. A handsome trophy was given for the tournament's winner by our old friend the landlord of the White Hart in St Teath, and Michael, mindful of my plaque-unveiling, was kind enough to ask me to make the presentation.

The tournament took place on 10 August 2003, just over two hundred and twenty-two years – a double-nelson – since the first recorded cricket in the field by the White Hart at St Teath. Grampound Road is emphatically a village, being a sort of satellite of nearby Grampound. Grampound is as definitely a town as Grampound Road is a village. In the seventeenth century Grampound was a rotten borough returning two Members of Parliament, including John Hampden, the great parliamentarian. It has an excellent smoked fish shop and both an Indian and a Chinese restaurant – sure indicators of civic status. Grampound does not, however, have a cricket club.

Grampound Road does. It may be on the poky side, and the day of the single-wicket knock-out the winner hit a six on to a roof behind the bowler's arm with nonachalant ease, but Grampound Road has a club good enough for the Cornish premiership.

We had been enduring an unprecedented heatwave, but by mid-afternoon when I arrived at the ground a slight chill was beginning to descend. Michael Williams's habitual jacket and tie suddenly seemed more appropriate than my own sockless shirtsleeve order.

Tea was being taken. Tea on occasions such as this never ceases to amaze, and this tea was duly amazing. I had lunched and taken no exercise so I made do with a mug of the traditional hot strong milky Indian tea in the equally traditional half-pint mug. I sat with Barry Burton, landlord of the White Hart in St Teath, who had donated a handsome silver cup for the winner and a friend of Michael Williams who had been in the audience at the du Maurier Festival the day the Bishop and Ronnie Harwood joined me to discuss cricket and writing. He was wearing a panama hat with a rhubarb and custard ribbon round it, and I wondered idly if the local lads who were competing in the competition knew – or cared – what it signified.

There were sixteen notional descendants of those eighteenth-century farmers competing for the 2003 trophy, and by the time I arrived all but four had been eliminated. The remaining contestants were Andrew Libby, just turned fifteen, who came from Roche and whose father, Clive, had been coaching him since he was knee high to a bee. Clive, who had come along to support his son, played for Cornwall and it looked as if his son was going to maintain a family tradition. Andrew's semi-final was against a robust-looking character called Ashley Morecome who, according to Michael Williams, was a last-minute entry and not supposed to be much of a cricketer, being more of a Penzance-Newlyn front-row forward. The other semi-final was between Rob Harrison, described to me by one onlooking supporter of his club, Newquay, as one of the best three all-rounders in the county. As Newquay, definitely a town as opposed to a village club, were top of the season's Cornish premiership, this sounded like a good recommendation. Michael Williams, on the other hand, tipped his opponent, a left-hander from Hayle named Lello, who had represented the county.

At this point, I'm sorry to say, television once more played a crucial role in my ability to record events. David decided, as he'd warned me, that he wanted to do an interview with me on the subject of single-wicket cricket, in the course of which I would evoke various names from the past, beginning with the eighteenth-century gentlemen who had played for the hat at St Teath and continuing through John Nyren and Lord Francis Beauclerk to E.V. Lucas and beyond.

What I hadn't realised was that in order to do the interview and make it plain to the viewers that I was actually present at a contemporary single-wicket tournament I would have to be filmed with the cricket going on in the background. This meant that I would have to sit facing the camera and with my back to the field of play. Half-way through the second game David asked me who my tip for the eventual winner was. Scrabbling through my notes but completely unaware of what was going on behind me, I said that my local expert Michael Williams had suggested the eventual winner would be Lello and that, bowing to his wisdom and erudition, I could only agree.

'Well you're both wrong,' said David, who had been watching the cricket over my shoulder as we talked, 'because he's just lost.'

I *was* able to watch the final, however, and thoroughly enjoyable it was. By the standards of what had gone before it was a positive marathon. The Williams rules, which bore little or no resemblance to those of John Nyren allowed two overs' batting apiece for the early rounds, three for the semi-finals, and a gruelling four for the final.

In the event Ashley Morecome, who batted first, did well to get to 41, but even though that was just over ten an over it never looked like being enough. Rob Harrison's powerful hitting was too much for the Penzance rugby player and he came out with a massive 71 runs, including several sixes, one of which fell smack on the slate roof of a house overlooking the ground.

I suppose the purists would say that the whole fast-paced affair was no more than a bucolic slog. Michael Williams, on the other hand, is a genuine cricket-lover, and when it comes to correctness of style and the importance of playing through the line with a straight bat he is as fierce a traditionalist as anyone. He thought the chaps batted beautifully and with all due orthodoxy. I was inclined to agree. I saw no cowshots.

On reflection it seemed an interesting and entirely legit-imate variation on the eleven-a-side game. Of course it was less of a team game than the ordinary form of cricket, but part of the game's attraction even when played between teams is that it includes any number of individual duels and encoun-ters within the context of collective team efforts.

Another aspect which I found appealing, especially as some-thing of a rabbit when it came to batting myself, was that you got more than one chance. If you played the rule of once out, out for ever, then some of the single-wicket games would be over almost before they began. In this tournament every time you were out you had six deducted from your total.

Under Williams rules there were six fieldsmen including a wicketkeeper as well as your opponent bowling. The bats-men were 'assisted' by a non-striking runner at the bowler's end. So although this was gladiatorial, head-to-head, one-on-one stuff there was still an element of teamwork involved. However, the emphasis was reversed, so that this was one man against another with a sub-text of assistance from others, whereas the team game is eleven against eleven with a thread of individual contest giving it added zest.

'Zest' was the word Michael used in his felicitous closing remarks and I must say that the occasion did seem to have a spring in its step and a sense of fun which didn't always seem to be there in games where league points were at stake. The result mattered, but not so much that it interfered with people's enjoyment.

I was reminded of a story which, a hundred or so years ago, E.V. Lucas said he heard between the innings of a village game and which he described then as 'the best single-wicket story of recent times that has come my way'. Even now it remains the best single-wicket story that has come *my* way in recent times as well.

The tale is that two elderly gents, both Old Blues – over eighty even in 1906 so they really were old – were so enthused by the University Match (that shows how long ago it was!) they arranged a single-wicket contest. On the appointed day they met with a number of sympathetic friends. B won the toss and batted, making 12 before being bowled (the Williams rule about each wicket scoring minus six had obviously not then been introduced). When it was A's turn to bat he was unable to do so. 'Anno Domini asserted itself. His weariness and weakness were too serious, he could only lie on a sofa and cry for his lost strength.'

Under the rules therefore B was entitled to go and bowl at A's undefended wicket. This he did while A lay at home 'in an agony of disappointment and feebleness'.

He needn't have agonised, however, for his friends suddenly returned with a disconsolate opponent.

'Bravo! Well played, old man!' they cried. 'You've won the match – he's bowled thirteen wides!'

Nothing as ridiculous happened at Grampound Road on the 222nd anniversary of the game for the 'silver laced hat', but you felt it almost could have done and that if it had Michael Williams would have quietly approved because it somehow reflected the timeless spirit of the game at its most quirky and quixotic.

As E.V. Lucas put it, compellingly, in *Fireside and Sunshine*, the single-wicket version of the game 'is a fiercer trial of all-round capacity than the ordinary game. The bowler has to bowl steadily without the rest offered by overs, and he must bat almost continuously after.'

He believed that a revival of the form was long overdue and much to be desired. I agree. Couldn't have put it better myself. Indeed I can hardly believe that he was writing in 1906.

'The MCC ought to think seriously of a single-wicket carnival at the end of each season. It is what cricket wants, and will want still more if the present commercial and over-strenuous conditions proceed by logical progression: a touch of irresponsibility, a breath of the sporting spirit. A few merry individual challenges sandwiched in between the formal rigours and classic austerities of the inter-county fixtures would save the first-class game. The Muse of Cricket just now, I believe, has a kinder feeling for the Saturday after-nooners on the village greens.'

It's a bit disconcerting, when trying not to sound like the archetypal old fart or Colonel Blimp, to realise that you are echoing sentiments expressed so lucidly and cogently almost a hundred years earlier. It seems incredible that anyone should have been deploring commercial considerations and creeping joylessness even before the beginning of the First World War, but there you have it. When I presented the Cup to the Cornish champion single-wicketeer, I found myself suggesting that a challenge should be issued to the foreigners across the Tamar and that England should send down a champion to do battle against the Cornish Number One. In doing so I was really only echoing sentiments expressed by E.V. Lucas in the first decade of the twentieth century. I suppose this is a mildly depressing thought.

★　★　★

Grampound Road is not a particularly pretty ground, nor come to that, is the village specially picturesque. Cornish villages don't tend to do thatch and honeysuckle and if your idea of a serious English cricketing village is based on *England, their England*, then Troon, the Duchy's most famous cricketing village, may come as a bit of a disappointment. Fordenden, the mythical village invented by A.G. Macdonell was in Kent and it was, you will remember, as if 'Ye Olde Englyshe Village' had been brought down from London to the country by special train complete with synthetic cobwebs, gaffers, dairymaids, an absent-minded vicar and a blacksmith who doubled up as the fast bowler. There were also red-roofed cottages, a flint church and a pub called the Three Horseshoes.

Perhaps I should not have mentioned 'special trains', for in 1972 when, in the first year of the Village Cup, the Troon First Eleven made it to Lord's, they hired a special train from West Cornwall to Paddington. Six hundred supporters booked tickets. But disaster struck. A tunnel near Dawlish collapsed and after a long wait the six hundred were sent home. Their side won, but that was scant consolation.

Anyway, although Troon is a place of indomitable spirit and character it did not seem, when I visited it, to be the stuff of which picture postcards are made. In fairness it should be said that I went on a dank, miserable day in January with a grey fog licking round the abandoned mine buildings and the terraced rows of workers' cottages. It felt more like a Lancashire League place – industrial rather than idyllic, though as in Lancashire the farms rub shoulders with the mines. It is no longer prosperous. When I first got in touch, Stephen White, the general secretary of the cricket club, introduced the place to me in a bleak sentence: 'It has been officially recognised by the Government as a deprived area,' he wrote, 'and Camborne-Redruth has the largest unemployment figures in the County.'

John Betjeman, in his *Shell Guide to Cornwall*, described it as a suburb of Camborne. I suspect this would not have gone down well with the inhabitants, who have a highly developed sense of independence. Betjeman went on to describe the village as 'a wide street of houses of dark stone with a tall Methodist chapel and a half-disused mission church hall and house of 1899 in a perpendicular style'.

He did not, unaccountably, mention the cricket club.

This seems to have been founded in 1875 though the club's historian acknowledges that 'little is known about those early years'. The team played on a field (there were two in the early days) near the village hotel at Croft Common. It sounds like a sporting pitch. The team rolled the wicket themselves, of course, with a roller made from Cornish granite and the long grass in the outfield was kept down with a hay-cutter. This was only partly effective and the preferred method of scoring was to hit the ball in the air rather than along the ground.

For obvious reasons their opponents were drawn from the local neighbourhood, with the great Derby match being the one against Camborne, the big smoke up the road. Their most distant opponents seem to have been the village of St Just, by Cape Cornwall, a few miles from Land's End. Away matches there involved a crack of dawn start and a long journey by horse-drawn bus.

In those early days the village, astonishingly, had two professional players, both of whom played for the county team as well. 'Kit' Trevarthen, who also played rugby for Cornwall, is usually described as a batsman but his most famous feat was as a bowler. At Lanhydrock, Trevarthen bowled Sir Jack Hobbs for a duck. Hobbs had not yet qualified for Surrey and was playing for his native Cambridgeshire. Trevarthen went on playing for Cornwall till 1934.

The other early Troon star was Ronald Vibart, who had been captain of cricket at Harrow and was an outstanding wicketkeeper–batsman. Vibart is generally described as 'colour-ful' and was reputed to enjoy a drink. He scored two centuries for Cornwall, but perhaps his finest hour was in Troon's epic victory against Truro. Truro, the home side, batted first and made 204 all out. Nothing had been seen or heard of Vibart for a full week before the game. When he did turn up he was extensively bandaged, the result, he explained, of having been involved in an argument with a glass door. Undaunted, he went out and made an unbeaten 112 as Troon passed the Truro total with flying colours. The whole match was over in four hours.

The first cricket leagues in Cornwall were formed in 1905. Troon joined in 1908, though it was 1947 before the First Eleven were to win their first championship (the Second Eleven won their league in the twenties). In 1926 the club moved to a new ground, a large field at Tresothlan Road, where they have remained ever since. For years they rented it from the local council but recently they were able to acquire the freehold.

The twenties and thirties were bad years for the village and the depression bit hard. Cricket was a welcome escape and although Troon were never champions they had some fine players, notably Len Lawry, a slow bowler who once took all ten wickets in an innings against the United Services. Another was Charlie Rickard, a left-handed batsman who had an auspicious debut for the county when he made 117 not out against a Kent Second Eleven which included Doug Wright in its attack.

Rickard was in the 1947 Troon side which won the League. That season he made over eight hundred and fifty runs. After clinching the Western League, they played the winners of the East for the title of champions of all Cornwall. They annihilated their opponents, scoring 307 for 2 of which Rickard made 134 not out.

The opening batsman that year was Jack Angove, who made more than four hundred runs. He opened for Troon and Cornwall and he was there in the club-house the other day when I visited the village. He still lives opposite the ground, only recently gave up being groundsman and is still the cricket secretary. His association with the club now extends over more than fifty years, though oddly he is not (quite) as Cornish as he sounds. He was actually born in the United States. The club likes to claim, tongue in cheek, that Jack was their first overseas player.

Troon took to the Village Cup as to the manner born. In the seventies they won at Lord's three times. The captain in those glory days was Terry Carter who, among many other captain's heroics, made a match-winning 79 not out in 1972 and won the match with a hooked six into the Tavern. He and his brother Brian went on to take the MCC coaching course. He was there that foggy morning, though his present job involves being away from home, and his involvement is now restricted to occasional outings for the Second Eleven. Brian, however, is still actively passing on his skills and is chairman of the youth committee. The club's current Monday evening coaching programme involves more than fifty boys between the ages of four and sixteen.

More to the point, however, they put out three adult teams every week as well as Under Sixteens, Thirteens and Elevens. Their best men are very good, and two Troon cricketers, for instance, went to Northants not long ago – Anthony Penberthy, whose father Gerald is club chairman, and David Roberts. The cricket ground has a fine modern score-board and 'arena seating' for several hundred. The club-house has a well-appointed bar, full-size snooker table and memorabilia galore, and is the focus for the social life of the community – including the darts and football teams. They don't owe anyone a penny and it costs just fifty pence a match to play, though players are expected to chip in a pound for tea. Club-house membership is an annual fiver.

Over the last few years they have entertained Somerset, Surrey, Notts and Northants for benefit matches, and speakers at the annual dinner have included the likes of Tom Graveney and Derek Randall – who scored a century at Troon when he came with his county.

To those who live east of the Tamar, Troon means the Scottish place where they play golf. Cricketing Troon is a far-away place of which they know nothing. The rules of the Village Cup stipulate that the population of the village should not exceed 2500. When I asked how many lived there the committee members said they always reckoned on about 2499.

Whatever the truth this is a remarkable club for such a community. Places ten or twenty times as big would be envious. It may be a long way from Lord's but, make no mistake, Troon Cricket Club is well and truly on the map.

Troon was going to play a big part in the TV series, but in the end it didn't. Something to do with fixtures, I think, though I wasn't entirely clear about it. However, we did film their annual dinner at the Porthminster Hotel in St Ives. I sat between two of the veterans who had played for the great team of the seventies – Gerald Dunstan and Jim Vincent. There were, almost, tears in their eyes as they described the thrill of walking through the Long Room at Lord's and down the steps where so many famous men had walked before. They were a great fielding side, they told me. After fielding practice their hands used to be so sore they would bathe them in the soothing waters of a nearby stream. They were, in a fine Cornish tradition, a great singing side as well.

This sort of cricket is still, I felt, played for fun. Glory occasionally, but fun comes first. On another occasion I was chatting to a twenty-year-old baker from Newlyn called Andrew Snell. Snell was also the Cornwall wicketkeeper. That morning he had started work at four a.m., knocked off at nine and driven directly to Boscawen Park in Truro in time to take part in the county's crucial game against Devon. 'Good mixture – baking and cricket!' he said.

I sensed a difference in attitude from the pros who play on the first-class circuit. He might not have been an inter-national sportsman but he baked for a living and he played for fun. I think it showed.

For most of my life I have lived near enough to Lord's to enjoy watching as much First Class (as opposed, some-times, to first-class) cricket as I wanted. Now, having moved to the far shore of the River Fowey, I find myself two hours at least from the nearest county championship ground. As a result I have been exposed, for the first time, to what, with horrid condescension, the English call Minor Counties cricket.

I've seen Cornwall play Warwickshire in a one-day

knock-out when they did adequately and would have done better, I thought, but for psychological inferiority. ('World Cup Stars coming to St Austell' was the dispiriting headline in the *Cornish Guardian*.) Cornwall's sprightly opening bowler, David Angove, was man of the match, and at 74 for 4 the Midlanders looked distinctly wobbly, only to be let off the hook. When Cornwall batted, their excellent opening pair saw off Gladstone Small and Shaun Pollock with apparent ease but then, once respectability had been achieved, I, for one, sensed a definite shrug of relief. Having escaped disgrace the Minor County felt able to subside without ignominy. A smidgeon more self-belief and they might have pulled off a surprise. Or so I thought. But perhaps that's wishful thinking and the gap between 'Minor Counties' and 'First Class' is as yawning as everyone says.

Some four thousand people attended the game, and the county secretary told me that, as a result, over £10,000 were sent to HQ. After their first-round match Lancashire, he told me, were unable even to scratch together a fraction of that. Cricket is alive and well in Cornwall. The secretary told me that at county level every age level was excellent. There are 96 clubs in the Cornish leagues putting out a total of some 190 teams. Supporters appear at least as numerous and knowledgeable as anywhere else in the United Kingdom. Now that I live here, cricket in the county doesn't seem in the least bit 'minor'.

In the summer of 2003 Cornwall played Kent at Truro in the third round of what is now the Cheltenham and Gloucester Trophy. In some ways it felt like a re-run of the game against Warwickshire. Kent were captained by Mark Ealham, a former Test cricketer, and included two others – Robert Key and the Australian Greg Blewett.

Cornwall batted first and were in all sorts of trouble, slumping to 90-odd for 8. There then followed two passages of play which certainly gave me pause for thought. First the final two Cornish wickets put on a hatful of runs, with two youngsters called Justin Stephens and Chris Hunkin hitting Kent all over the place. I thought Hunkin looked particularly good, driving the quick bowlers hard and straight for classic looking boundaries. When Kent batted they eventually sauntered home but not before losing four wickets, two of them to Hunkin who conceded only nineteen runs off his allotted ten and had Blewett in all sorts of trouble before finally getting him out. It was no surprise when Hunkin was made man of the match — the second time I had seen a Cornishman made man of the match in a game against a first-class county.

You may well now be asking what this has to do with village cricket and the answer is that Hunkin's club was Grampound Road and Grampound Road is a village. Actually, as we've seen, it's a sort of adjunct to Grampound, which is technically a town, having once been the rotten borough that returned John Hampden to Parliament. Justin Stephens, who also did well, played for St Buryan, another place which is unquestionably a village. It is a very faraway settlement being west of Penzance. David Cornwell alias John le Carré lives in a house on the cliffs nearby.

Both these villages were, at the time of writing, in the Cornish Premier League and doing well. Meanwhile unquestioned towns such as Penzance, St Austell, Camborne, Launceston and Bude were one or even two divisions below.

Which brings me back to my earlier hypothesis that what we call 'village cricket' is more a state of mind than a function of size. I suspect that what villages such as St Buryan and Grampound Road were playing was not 'village cricket' in the accepted sense, whereas the game as played by Launceston and Bude might have been. Confusing.

5

Local Heroes Go to Lord's

I hadn't originally intended to write so much about Cornish cricket but I'm glad to have done so, partly because it is now 'cricket on my doorstep' and partly because, like so many things Cornish, it seems much more English than the rest of the United Kingdom. I am aware that this is a paradox, for Cornwall prides itself on being a place apart, an ancient Celtic kingdom which barely accepts that it is part of the United Kingdom let alone part of England. Nevertheless I do believe that 'The Duchy' is one of the most English of counties in the sense that it is one of the most traditional.

This is partly a function of remoteness and partly of poverty. Despite cheap Ryanair flights to and from Newquay airport and improvements to the rail and road systems Cornwall is still, by British standards, a long way from London or even Bristol. Foreigners, especially Americans, think this is ridiculous – 'Orlando is further from us than you are from London,' said an acquaintance in Miami when I was there recently. This is perfectly true, but the British are convinced that London and Cornwall are at opposite ends of the earth. I know proud Cornish men and women who have not been to London or even crossed the Tamar for twenty or thirty years. It is a boast, a badge they wear with pride.

Londoners reciprocate. 'How nice to see you,' said a journalist acquaintance at the Ritz media party in July 2003, 'but I thought you were in Cornwall.' He said it as if the possibility of moving between one and the other place was a physical impossibility. Through gritted teeth I explained that I had come up on the train and that it was possible by catching the sleeper to leave home in time to be in London for breakfast, do a full day's work, finished off with a prolonged dinner and then, by catching the return sleeper, be home by seven o'clock the following morning. I'd be at my desk before he would.

I don't think he believed me. The distance is as much psychological as real.

The relative poverty means that the Cornish, more than other inhabitants of the Kingdom, are inclined to make their own pleasures. Thus, in part, the high incidence of amateur dramatic clubs, bands, choirs, rugby and, yes, cricket clubs.

I could have written even more about Cornish cricket if I had tied myself more closely to the television series David and Laura were making. The more we went on, however, the more we diverged, following ever more different agenda.

Originally I suggested that we should film the two clubs in Cornwall and Devon that I originally wanted to focus on, namely Boconnoc and Chagford. David agreed to these but, as described, Boconnoc had to go quite early in the proceedings. The TV substitute was Werrington, just to the north of Launceston right up on the Devon border. Werrington made a good stand-in for Boconnoc as it too had begun life in the nineteenth century as a feudal estate team manned originally by a mixture of squire's family from the great house, the Williamses, and men and boys who worked on the estate and farms.

Similar changes had taken place, so that although there was still a Williams (Mike) in Werrington Park there were far fewer estate workers or tenant farmers to draw on. The standard of cricket was much higher than at Boconnoc and the team had even on one famous occasion got as far as the Lord's final of the Village Cup. The Launceston Cricket Club, which shared its ground with the prospering and successful local rugby club, was not as good as Werrington and one rather felt that Werrington was creaming off the best of the local Launceston talent. There was a particular family called Smeeth which seemed to have more than its fair share of gifted cricketers in every generation.

Mike Williams, the club patron, was the nephew of Julian Williams of Caerhays Castle, a wonderful Gothic Nash-built edifice on the south coast with one of the great plant-hunters' gardens, full of amazing rhododendrons, azaleas and magnolias. Julian had been president of the Cornwall County Cricket Club since 1967 as well as of the local Gorran Haven village club. He had some entertaining anecdotes about players of the past, including the one who habitually bowled while smoking a pipe. Another had a wooden leg. There was no doubting the Williamses' love of cricket, though, I felt they, like E.V. Lucas, were happier in the pavilion than at the crease.

Like Boconnoc the Werrington ground is in the middle of nowhere. Many people had told me it was a vision of loveliness, but I didn't actually think it was a patch on Boconnoc apart from the fact that there were breathtaking views of Dartmoor away to the east on the far side of the Tamar. Otherwise it was just a tad plain and, as perhaps befits a side in the Cornish first division (though not the top division because they have a Premiership sponsored by 'Jolly's Drinks' like all the other Cornish divisions), the playing area is surrounded by advertising hoardings. There are none of those at Boconnoc and I'm sure the Fortescues would forbid them.

Every community and every club is unique, but if one was dealing in categories or genre Boconnoc and Werrington would feature on the same list. Cornish Feudal.

It was the same with several other Cornish villages. I had suggested Troon for TV because they had been nationally victorious in the past and also because they were so unlike the stereotype, such a vivid contrast to a place like Boconnoc. David Taylor's other choice was Paul, which is effectively the inland part of the parish of Mousehole, one of the quaintest and most picturesque of all Cornish fishing villages. Mousehole provided most if not all of the crew of the ill-fated Penlee lifeboat, which sank with all hands in a dreadful winter storm in 1989.

John Betjeman has a succinct description of Paul: 'The church town, on the high hill inland, is a granite village with

1760 almshouses. In the church is a Victorian tomb to Dolly Pentreath of Mousehole who died in 1777 aged ninety-one and was said to be the last speaker of Cornish. The church (St Pol de Leon) has low box pews, barrel ceilings, seventeenth- and eighteenth-century monuments and an east window in blues and purples by Anning Bell.'

David went for Paul largely because he had discovered, while making a series about the Church in Cornwall, that Paul, despite being a modest little village, put on a nativity play with a cast of a hundred and twenty. I had some sympathy with this, but wondered whether Paul was a little too like Troon – a tight, remote community of which the cricket club is the thriving central hub and focus.

Should you catch the TV series and always assuming the scene doesn't end up on the cutting room floor, you will see Mr and Mrs Heald attended the Paul annual fund-raising duck regatta and the cricket club's euchre drive. You will see the Mid Level On Air Talent (what I would have been called if the television series had been shot in the United States) picking the winning duck in the last race and being presented with a magnificent lunch hamper includ-ing wine, chicken and clotted cream. This could have been an embarrassing problem. Thank God for the Hutchins Alms Houses, endowed under the will of a local lad who died in 1709 after making a fortune from sugar and slaves or some such. The Alms Houses are still going strong and I was next to the chairman of the Trustees when my duck came in, breasting the tape after a frantic charge down the mighty River Trungle which flows through the village and down which fifty bright yellow plastic ducks came bobbing along at regular intervals throughout the morning. I hadn't a clue what to do with the basket of goodies, though I did know that the one thing the visiting Talent couldn't do was waltz off with the first prize.

'Give it to us,' whispered the chairman, so after the last race we walked up to the Alms Houses, which are now well-appointed sheltered housing flats. The warden seemed pleased with the unexpected largesse so I walked on to the King's Arms for lunch and euchre. The pub was warm, full and very much the centre of village and cricket activity. The newish landlord had just joined the Hutchins trustees and was clearly fitting in well. His support for the cricket team was well judged, for there was a regular running suggestion that it would be a good idea to install a bar in the pavilion. This was always vetoed, partly because the ground was outside the village and there would be problems with drink-driving, partly because a licensed bar might encourage theft, but most of all because it would be unfair on such a friendly publican.

The euchre, which is a card game a bit like whist, was noisy, fast and, to me, only marginally comprehensible. The Cornish insist that it is an exclusively Cornish game. The Cornish are inclined to say this about a number of things, such claims being, I think, a manifestation of Cornish pride or even, whisper it softly, of Cornish insecurity. One of our partners – we played in fours – who worked at the Royal Naval Air Station at Culdrose – said that he had come across the game in Kent. My wife said that she had learned it from her granny in South Australia, but we all agreed that this was virtually a Cornish colony, thanks to the emigration of Cousin Jacks to the tin and copper mines down under. The man from Culdrose said that, as its name suggested, the game was of French origin and had been imported by prisoners of war in Napoleon's time. Hence its popularity along the entire south coast. Our Cornish partner looked sceptical about this, but I had noticed a number of French names around the place – a Gruzelier in the churchyard, an Ambrose de Rouffignac on the War Memorial. The memorial to Dolly Pentreath, the last Cornish-speaker, was erected by Prince Louis Lucien Bonaparte. I was not surprised to find euchre being played in the pub and I was inclined to support the French theory. However, being in a Cornish pub among Cornishmen I judged it better to keep quiet.

That's enough Cornwall for the book, though David and his TV crew continued to follow the fortunes of Paul throughout the year. They had a good season, thankfully, though there appeared to be a bit of a feud between two of the leading village cricket families – the Snells and the Osbornes. This involved one of them giving up the captaincy and defecting to Penzance. In Division One the team beat their old rivals Werrington at home but lost away. In the Village Cup they became regional champions before coming up against a jazzy Oxfordshire outfit from Shipton-under-Wychwood. They played them at home the same day that I was speaking at the Fowey anniversary cricket lunch, and rain stopped play when Paul were having a tough time with the bat. The replay was fixed for Shipton-under-Wychwood – an expensive and time-consuming trip, and a daunting prospect as the Oxfordshire team were the reigning champions. Paul were right to be daunted. They lost.

And so to Glorious Devon.

I was already forming the opinion that the similarities between village cricket clubs were far greater than the differences – provided, that is, that the club had not become extinct like Martock and others. Devon, so very unlike its western neighbour in so many respects, rather reinforced my view. Thatch and red soil against slate and granite. Anglo-Saxon against Celt, agriculture against mining . . . the two counties really are chalk and cheese, but when it came to cricket they looked very similar. The most obvious differences – and they are dwindling – is that Devon is closer to London and a lot more prosperous.

Almost the first comment someone made when I arrived at the Chagford Cricket Club on the edge of Dartmoor was, 'I couldn't bear to live where you do!'

'Why not?'

'Because you can't get up to Lord's and back in a day.'

For a certain sort of cricket-lover this is an essential consideration. Exeter, which is within a spit of Chagford, is two hours by train from Paddington; my nearest station is more like four and a half. The sleeper introduces an interesting element into the equation, but for the sort of cricket supporter who likes to set out after breakfast in his blazer and panama with a hamper and binoculars and be home in time for dinner Cornwall is no use whatever, whereas parts of Devon most certainly are. And I quickly formed the impression that the blazer and panama, hamper and binocular quotient in Chagford was unusually high.

Another slightly unkind judgement on Chagford in Devon is that if you were to erect a high wall around it no one would notice. I heard this remark from a Chagfordian, albeit a relative newcomer with only a decade or so of residence to his credit, and I'm still not quite sure whether it's a barbed reference to the world's indifference to this remote, easy-paced place or whether it reflects on the introspection and insularity of those who live there. Either way I certainly get the impression that the relationship between Chagford and the world at large is pretty distant.

The most obvious exception to this is the cricket ground.

'This is where God meant cricket to be played,' says Chagford Cricket Club's chairman, Bryce Rundle. He does not say this boastfully or humorously but as a plain matter of fact. Looking across from the memorial seats (one dedicated to a former Chagford postman, another to a one-time Chagford vicar) you can't help agreeing. The backdrop is the Dartmoor fringe: the steep green bracken-covered slopes of Nattadon Hill to the left and Meldon Hill to the right climb up to sublime granite-spotted summits. It is the backdrop against which Chagford has played its cricket since 1895 if not before.

The scenery is unquestionably magnificent, but it is not this which makes the Chagford ground so unexpected. I would have imagined a small sporting field with slopes and bumps and the sort of idiosyncracies worth priceless runs and wickets to the home side, but Chagford's ground is, as the *Great Little Chagford Book* proclaims, 'as flat as East Anglia'. It is also enormous and the wicket is nurtured with sufficient love and care to make the ground good enough for Devon to play county cricket on. In fact I've seen first-class grounds with a dodgier surface.

The invaluable *Great Little Chagford Book* confirms that it was not always thus. Indeed says its author, Chips Barber, 'visiting soccer and cricket teams must have thought the playing surface was simply a continuation of Dartmoor as the Padley Common's War Memorial Fields venue left a lot to be desired.' The first ground was a bog, then the team moved across the hedge to another field known as the Adder Pit which was as sporting as its predecessor, and then came the dramatic translation to the present Elysian Field.

I chose Chagford because of the president and my

godmother. The president, Tim Dudman, is an old friend of my family's. He was involved with my father in a number of almost invariably abortive business ventures in the sixties which always seemed to demand a lot of lunch. My godmother is mildly mystified by Dudman and given to asking in a sceptical way, 'What exactly was Tim doing, selling Horlicks in the Cameroons?' He and his late wife Diana moved to Devon from London some years ago. My godmother has lived in Devon since her late husband Mike retired from his job as a Provincial Commissioner in Nyasaland. For many years they lived in Moretonhampstead, a few miles from Chagford, but moved to a more convenient house in downtown Chagford in the nineties. Cricket is not really her game, but writing about her local club provided a welcome opportunity to stay the occasional night at her place. Besides she knows everyone in Chagford, including the cricketers.

It was she who introduced me to the principal architect of the modern Chagford amphitheatre, her friend Steve Pefanis, who as his name suggests is of Greek origin, though he actually comes from South Africa. After a pre-war apprenticeship with Imperial Airways Pefanis spent all his life in international aviation, finishing as number two with IATA. He and his wife had got to know the area because her sister's family farms locally. They always loved this corner of Devon and retired here in the late seventies.

He always promised himself he would have an active retirement and also that he would try to contribute to the life of the community. The first project that caught his attention was tennis. The existing courts were in poor nick and together with a supportive neighbour he formed a Recreational Trust. Once the tennis courts had been rebuilt and the Trust firmly established he turned his attention to 'The Field'. He had never played cricket or football, but he could see that the existing grounds were hopelessly primitive. Somehow, mainly because 'I went round twisting arms', he raised about £100,000 and set about building a ground on what was in effect a marsh with a fully fledged stream running slap across the middle.

'I supervised the whole construction myself,' he says. 'The bog was about twelve foot deep and we had to dig out 3,300 cubic metres of peat. The whole thing was done in three months. The biggest cost was buying the Surrey loam for the square, which was laid to the very highest professional standards. The work was all done by volunteers. The final compacting was done by old-fashioned "heeling". I was practically humming "cha-cha-cha" to the volunteers,' he says. 'When dusk came I brought my car down and shone the lights on the pitch. It was a brilliant way to pick out any undulations.'

A year or so ago he managed to organise another £200,000 to build a spanking new two-storey pavilion, which has not only been a great bonus for the cricketers and footballers but also a place for the whole community. It can be hired out for weddings and parties of all kinds. The most recent venture has been the refurbishment of the sheds for the mowers and rollers. That was £25,000. Not a problem. He and Dudman raised it in a fortnight.

The creation of the ground was reward enough in itself, but he has also acquired a genuine enthusiasm for the game. It also gave him 'one of the happiest and most magical days of my life'. This was the day Chagford played Soweto. The South African cricketer, Fanie de Villiers, was playing in Torquay nearby and Pefanis went to see him to discuss some kind of collaboration. De Villiers mentioned that the Soweto team was touring England and suggested that Pefanis get in touch with the South African cricket supremo, Dr Ali Bacher. As a result the highlight of the Chagford centenary was Soweto *v.* Chagford on Friday 21 July 1995.

'It was quite a culture shock for Chagford,' he says. 'They beat the hell out of us on the field but afterwards everyone was impeccably behaved. We held a barbecue and we created three precedents. First they sang wonderful South African songs and then Chagford replied in kind with their own Devonian and Cornish songs. Second the Sowetans were all put up in local people's homes. And third we raised money on site to help with the costs of the tour.'

It was an exceptionally friendly event and celebrations continued far into the night. Three of the Sowetan players were called Justice, Peace and Harmony – Justice Nkutha, Peace Nkutha and Harmony Ntshinga. This prompted one wag to wonder if they wouldn't be joined by Faith, Hope and Charity in nine months' time.

Tim Dudman suggested I come over for the friendly game against Kenn, a village the other side of the A38 near Exeter racecourse. It wouldn't be quite the jamboree of the Soweto match but it's a very old fixture on the Chagford list with two appropriately ancient skippers for the day – Pete Murfin, the Kenn captain, was in his late fifties, while Mike Wreford, his Chagford opposite number, was sixty-seven and still going strong.

We had lunch in the president's garden on the slopes of Nattadon Hill. This was a well lubricated affair, culminating in coffee and calvados, and play was well established by the time the president, I and the president's dog set off on foot down the hillside.

Chagford were batting and there was a loud Kenn appeal as we paused behind the sight-screen at the bowler's end. 'Not out,' called the president loudly. The umpire agreed. Tim then introduced me to chairman Bryce Rundle and the three of us contemplated the flat broad acres. A couple of years ago in order to comply with Minor County regulations the club added another twenty metres to the playing surface. There is even a tree on the field of play just like Canterbury. It's an oak.

'It's bloody difficult to get the boys to play away from home these days,' said Bryce. Other grounds and facilities simply don't measure up. Today's game was a friendly, but the previous year Chagford joined the Devon League. They won Division 'E' at the first attempt and were going well in Division 'D'. The leagues, as in so many places, were a source of continuing debate. 'You get some effing and blinding on the pitch,' he conceded, 'but it's all OK in the bar.' League cricket here, as elsewhere, gives games a competitive edge, but some players, especially the older ones, think it can make players over-competitive. In village cricket round here a batsman always 'walked' if he knew he was out. Now, increasingly, they stand their ground.

Bryce is a Chagford boy who went away and came home. He was with the NatWest bank, worked in London, then came back west as Area Personnel Manager in Exeter. Like Stephen Pefanis he is energetic and resourceful. For example, they have an extremely impressive array of weight training gear in the gym. They got it for next to nothing because it used to be in Dartmoor Prison not far away and the prison was getting rid of it in exchange for some brand new stuff which actually turned out to be not nearly as good.

Out in the middle the game was looking pretty one-sided. The Chagford openers, David Steele and Paul Ridgers, put on 122 – the first opening century partnership of the season – and didn't look in much trouble. It's a very placid, true sort of wicket. So much so that in the whole day's play only three players were bowled and there wasn't a single lbw. All the other wickets were caught or stumped.

It wasn't until Simon Snell came on as third change that the wickets started to fall. Snell took four including a catch off his own bowling. Eventually Chagford declared at tea on 198 for 5.

Tea was a serious Devon cream number. Out in the middle another Chagford stalwart, Michael Bennett, sometime captain of Worcester College, Oxford, was sweeping the wicket. He used to be with the education authority in Coventry but took early retirement after a nasty car crash on the motorway. He and Bryce share responsibility for the wickets and there are serious lines of demarcation which are never discussed. 'I think,' mused Michael, 'that he prefers me to use the rollers. He did paint the lines yesterday but only because I was at Lord's. I haven't cut a wicket for three years.'

'The lines here are much more precisely drawn than at Lord's,' said Bryce.

After tea Kenn batted. The veteran Mike Wreford opened the bowling. His club captain, Nick Rowe, had said rather unkindly, when he was recalled to the league side, that 'he's very round-arm these days', but he looked pretty chipper to me. It wasn't long before he got one past his opposite number, Pete Murfin, who was on 11 at the time. There was a loud appeal and without a moment's hesitation Murfin tucked his bat under his arm and walked off, giving a little nod of acknowledgement to Wreford as he walked past. Later Wreford

told me the umpire was about to give Murfin 'not out' as
he couldn't be sure. 'The only two players who would have
known for sure,' said Wreford, 'were Pete and the wicket–
keeper. If only all cricket was played like this.'

I sat and chatted. Michael said the wicket was 'low and
slow' which was hardly surprising as it had to contend with
seventy thousand gallons of water streaming off Meldon Hill
every year. Pete Murfin, the Kenn skipper, was looking slightly
piqued after his dismissal. He was obviously a man who didn't
like getting out. He knew it was a perfectly fair dismissal but
if anything that made it even worse. He said that he actually preferred playing on the old Adder Pit because it was so
soggy that it was easy on the feet, whereas this new immaculately drained surface gave you foot-ache. Meanwhile his
son David was looking useful until the ageless Wreford bowled
him on 41. Earlier in the year Murfin *père et fils* had shared
in a double century stand – an all-time Kenn record. If Pete
could hang in for another decade or so he reckoned there
could be three generations of Murfin playing in the team.
His grandson was presently three years old.

Around six o'clock pints of beer appeared as if by magic.
I sipped and studied the fixture list. Totnes, Dawlish,
Babbacombe and Buckfastleigh in the Devon League; a
friendly against the Britannia Royal Naval College sponsored
by the Chagford Dental Practice and another against the
Metropolitan Mounted Police sponsored by the Old Forge
Tea Rooms.

From a distance the batting looked better than the bowling, but the wickets continued to fall, thanks in part to some
nifty wicketkeeping by Graham Howard, who had two catches
and a couple of stumpings; and when the last man came in
Kenn were 108 for 9 and the game looked over. Mike

Wreford had taken four wickets but now, surprisingly, neither he nor anyone else could take the final wicket. The last two Kenn men put on a sprightly 37 and were undefeated at the close when Kenn were 54 runs short of what would have been a highly improbable victory. Honours therefore more or less even.

A fortnight later I came back for a drinks party given by the president for all his surviving predecessors. It was a convivial affair in a tent in his garden. The presidents seemed a jolly if mixed bunch. Not many clubs like Chagford could claim an American, let alone Paul Henderson, proprietor of the celebrated Gidleigh Park Hotel nearby. Simon Butler, the Harrovian president in centenary year, had once played rugby and cricket for East Africa. The secretary, John Middleditch, turned out to have been at school with me, though we both completely failed to recognise or even remember each other.

Afterwards my godmother, the Pefanises and the Bowaters, who run a succesful holiday cottage business, adjourned for fish and chips in the Bullers Arms, named after Sir Redvers Buller, the Boer War general (it had previously been the Baker's Arms). After a while most of the other former presidents came in and gathered round the bar, looking as if they were set for a long discursive evening, but godmother, who after all was nearing eighty, and I made our excuses and left.

Next morning before breakfast I clambered up Meldon and came back over the cricket ground. It was deserted now apart from a couple of dog-walkers, but it still looked vast, beautiful and billiard-table smooth. Evelyn Waugh, who disliked cricket as much as his brother Alec loved it, wrote *Brideshead Revisited* in Chagford. Not many people know that. That novel, however, was about a romantic sort of England that he thought was lost and gone for ever. Appropriate

therefore that this miraculous cricket Oval should have
suddenly been born and breathed new life into this otherwise somnolent seeming little town. (No, it's not technically
a village because it's an ancient Stannary town, but it *feels*
like a village.) If you did build that high wall round the place
they'd still have as good a ground as any in Devon. I think
I'd notice it had gone missing.

If I had stuck to my original scheme of one ground per
county, Chagford would have been it. Television, however,
required a second ground to represent Devon and between
us we chose Clyst St George, just south of Exeter. It has
become a virtual suburb or dormitory for the cathedral city,
but when the cricket club began it was very much a separate community, dominated by a mansion – Pytte House –
and a squirarchical family – the Gibbs. The Gibbs made a
fortune out of guano, after which some of them went off to
the Bristol area, where they built Tynesfield, one of the greatest of all Victorian houses, now acquired by the National
Trust, and in 1928 acquired a barony.

The Gibbs who stayed at home seem to have started the
cricket club at Clyst St George in 1894. There are no records
until 1903, when A.H. Gibbs is recorded as both president
and captain. In 1907 he was succeeded by another Gibbs,
the Revd W.C.A.H., however, retained the captaincy, relin-
quishing it on the outbreak of the First World War, only to
be reappointed on his return as Major Gibbs in 1919. Ah
those majors and those vicars long ago, long ago. What a vital
contribution they made to cricket in the shires.

Another Major, H.G. Shrubb, who was agent for the estate,
was president for many years until he was succeeded by
Freddie Brimblecombe some time after the Second World

War. Brimblecombe continued as president until his early death in 1992.

At this point in the Clyst St George narrative I felt I had stumbled on something. Brimblecombe is a moderately common name in the West Country, but Freddie Brimblecombe seemed likely to be a rarer commodity. I had a feeling that my mother had talked about a 'Freddie Brim' back in the Martock days of her childhood.

Yes, she confirmed, Dr Brimblecombe was the local GP and a great friend of her father, my grandfather, the Martock team scorer. 'Freddie Brim', his son, was my mother's first boyfriend, though the most exotic thing they ever did together was to smoke a cigarette in the raspberry cage in the garden of 'The Green'. My family's glove business went bust, my grandfather died and my mother and Freddie lost touch. She knew, however, that he, like his father, had become a doctor and moved to the Exeter area. A few years earlier she had read his obituary in *The Times*. He and the former president of the Clyst St George Cricket Club sounded like one and the same.

There was a Brimblecombe in the local phone book and it turned out to be Freddie's widow. I went to see her and Freddie's daughter and spent a happy afternoon listening to them yarning on about the old boy and the happy times he had spent with his beloved cricketers. He himself had been educated at school at Blundells, the Tiverton public school, and never much excelled at the game, but came to love it with a passion. He inaugurated a special president's tea with much food and drink and some jolly cricket. A world-class paediatrician, with a special interest in the Sudan, he had refused all blandishments from the great London teaching hospitals and remained a professor in Exeter. Cricket and the 'craic' that went with it obviously provided a relaxation, not least because of the mildly eccentric mix of characters who played. One was 'Olly', a porter at Exeter St David's railway station. The Brimblecombes always received fantastic service when they boarded the London train.

Part of the essence of true village cricket is its haphazard and localised nature, but not everyone sees it like that. After a hundred years or so the habit of just playing your neighbours and a handful of visitors in fancy hats can begin to pall. At least it can for some. Besides, village cricketers can dream. Most men who have ever put bat to ball will have dreamed of performing on a more glamorous stage than the village green.

This, more or less, was what Ben Brocklehurst thought at the beginning of the seventies.

Brocklehurst played village cricket for Budleigh Salterton from the age of twelve. Budleigh Salterton is actually a Devonian town not far from Clyst St George with a population recorded in my admittedly out-of-date gazetteer as 3,957 and it's more famous for its croquet than for any other game. However, as far as Brocklehurst is concerned Budleigh Salterton plays village cricket. Or did in the thirties when he was in his teens.

I first became aware of him in my prep school days at Connaught House when he captained Somerset. They weren't very good. In fact in Brocklehurst's brief stay, from 1952 to 1954, they finished bottom of the championship every year. That old Somerset character R.C. Robertson-Glasgow even wrote in the *Cricketer* magazine, which Brocklehurst was later to own, that there was a threat of Somerset leaving the first-class game altogether. 'Crusoe' recalled a game in his own playing days when his team-mate, Tom Young, approached from cover-point one miserable Thursday morning and said, 'I make the crowd twenty-four – twenty-three really cos one of them died overnight.'

It seems a bit unfair to recall that while with Somerset Brocklehurst scored just 1671 runs in 110 innings for an average of 15.91, and as a bowler managed just the one wicket for 36 runs. Listening to him talk you certainly get the impression that it was a tricky dressing-room to control and the wickets weren't always up to much. There was one dreadful day in Weston-super-Mare when the veteran Bertie Buse's benefit match was all over in a day. The wicket was, according to Brocklehurst, 'covered in stones and acorns'.

Nevertheless, before he went off to farm in Berkshire, Brocklehurst did manage some notable coups off the field of play – the most significant of which was hiring the amazing Bill Alley. Brocklehurst found him playing league cricket up in Blackpool and persuaded him to come south to Taunton. No one knew exactly how old Alley was, but he was certainly over forty when he did the double in 1961. Between 1957 and 1968 Alley scored over 16,000 runs for Somerset, and took 738 wickets and 267 catches. If Ben Brocklehurst's contribution to Somerset's playing record was a shade marginal he deserves a place in their hall of fame for bringing them Bill Alley.

After farming Brocklehurst went into journalism and found himself with a stable of magazines which included the grand old *Cricketer* magazine. It wasn't particularly profitable. In fact not at all profitable. His chairman advised him to close it down, but he refused. The ubiquitous Jim Swanton who was editing the magazine responded to two years of losses by demanding extra pages. The demand was met and the magazine staggered on.

The original seed for what was to become the National Village Cricket Championship, better known as the Village Cup, came from Aidan Crawley. Crawley was a Corinthian cricketer of distinction, a Labour MP in the forties, a Conservative one in the sixties, president of London Weekend Television but, more important, president of MCC.

In 1970 Crawley asked Brocklehurst and Swanton to lunch at Lord's to discuss ways in which the *Cricketer* could promote the National Cricket Association. After lunch Crawley, no doubt recollecting days of glory in his cavalier cricket-playing youth, gazed out of the committee room windows and declared that he had often thought of two village sides playing on this most historic of all cricket grounds. Reading through the old score-books at Arundel, I found that Crawley once made 147 in 55 minutes playing for the Duke of Norfolk's XI against Lord Eldon's team. The very next day he made 164 in 77 minutes. No wonder Crawley felt misty-eyed at the thought of village teams doing something similar at cricket's holy of holies. I think that as he looked out at the green green grass of Lord's he was indulging in a little wishful retrospection. If only . . .

Crawley's sentiments may have been no more than a murmur of wistful thinking but they took root in Brocklehurst's receptive mind. Back in the *Cricketer* office in Kent he summoned his general manager, Harry Constantine, to discuss how they might translate Crawley's pipe-dream into reality. Brocklehurst decided, in the arbitrary way one would expect from a former Somerset captain, that he would initiate a competition between proper cricketing villages. A 'proper' village should consist of a rural community of not more than 2,500 inhabitants surrounded by open countryside. Nowadays you'd be able to access such places on the

Internet. In 1970, however, the Internet didn't exist, so Brocklehurst had to identify suitable villages by using the AA book. Once this had been done they did manage to get the addresses organised on a neighbour's computer, but even so the standard letters were sent off to the village pub or, failing that, the village garage.

Some time around now a piece of serendipitous personal coincidence came into play because Ben Brocklehurst apparently turned up at my family home to discuss his ideas for a cricket world cup with my father. My father had left the Army in 1956 and after a chequered few years helping to start the Duke of Edinburgh's Award Scheme, joining a film production company, trying his hand at import-export and various other marginal and financially iffy projects, had found a relatively safe harbour as the Manager of Special Events at W.D. and H.O. Wills, the Bristol-based cigarette manufacturers. Wills sponsored sundry horse-racing, Douglas Bunn's show-jumping arena at Hickstead, power-boat racing and much else besides. Brocklehurst reckoned they were a sensible target for his scheme and accordingly approached my father. The two evidently got on well. My father may not have been one of the great cricketers, but he was temperamentally well-disposed to the idea. It looked like a runner but, alas, in the summer of 1972 he was killed in a car crash and the notion of a co-operation between Wills and the *Cricketer* died with him.

That did not, however, mean the end of the Brocklehurst-Crawley dream. From the offices of the *Cricketer* magazine a letter was sent out to as many 'villages' as Brocklehurst and Constantine could identify. Over a thousand recipients responded, and after sorting, sifting and general weeding out, eight hundred villages were included in the initial draw. Not unreasonably Brocklehurst now approached the NCA, at whose Lord's lunch the idea had originally been mooted, to find out if they could help with the obviously complex and time-consuming task of administration. The NCA, to its discredit, played the ball straight back to the bowler. Sorry, old boy. Too big a deal; don't have the resources. So Brocklehurst found himself slightly hoist with his own petard. He had come up with this brilliant idea but now he had to make it work.

As David Demelman points out in his official history of the first twenty years' of the competition, it was tempting to simply put all eight hundred names into an enormous hat – preferably lined or trimmed with silver – and pull the names out just as in the draw for any cup. The problem with that approach was that the *Cricketer* was dealing with villages of a few hundred souls and bank balances to match. All very well for Manchester United to travel to Plymouth for a cup-tie, but not so good for Bishops Lydeard to travel from Somerset to Mawdsley in the heart of Lancashire.

The solution was for the competition to be arranged on a regional basis, either county by county or, where a single county could not muster enough entrants, by grouping, say, Hereford and Worcester together. There would then be a series of regional rounds over ever-increasing areas until ultimately two finalists emerged and played their deciding match at the holy of holies, Lord's itself.

As far as the games were concerned they were to be played over forty overs a side unless the two captains agreed otherwise or, of course, one side was bowled out within the allotted span. In first-class cricket forty overs, which was the span of the Sunday afternoon Benson and Hedges matches, was considered a bit of a tip-and-run, here-today-gone-tomorrow, basically unserious thrash. Speaking now from an entirely personal point of view, I would like to say that if you are getting on in years, don't play much, are not especially sound in wind and limb, and are fielding on a hot or muggy day, then forty overs feels like a timeless Test.

Bowlers were limited to a maximum of nine overs apiece, which meant that the fielding side had to use at least five bowlers. This latter condition would still apply if the match was curtailed, because the rules stipulated that no bowler could bowl more than a quarter of the total number of overs.

The side scoring the most runs, irrespective of the number of wickets lost, automatically won. In the event of a tie the side losing the fewer wickets won the match. If that didn't work then the side receiving the fewer balls won, and if there was still an impasse the winner was the side which scored more runs after twenty overs. If all this failed then they had to revert to the bowling competition which, as David Demelman points out, is cricket's equivalent of the penalty shoot-out. And strange things can happen. *Vide* the E. V. Lucas single-wicket match in which one of the contestants bowled thirteen wides at an unprotected wicket. All pretty straightforward.

The first sponsors of the Village Cup were Haig whisky, who lasted six years. It seems appropriate for a booze company to sponsor the competition although, surely, the true village cricketer's tipple is beer or cider, at least until after stumps. There were 795 competitors in that first year, the first of them being Welford Park in Berkshire and the 750th Snelling from Kent, which county provided more contestants than any other, with no fewer than fifty-eight. As the *Cricketer*'s offices were in the same county this seemed only right.

As we have already seen, Troon of Cornwall were the first

champions, and worthy ones at that. They beat four Cornish sides before coming up against Evercreech of Somerset, who were all out for 142 in pursuit of Troon's 145 for 6. In the next round they had an easy win against Shillingstone, the Dorset champions, before very nearly coming unstuck against Bledlow. Bledlow made 204 for 5, but Troon just made it past that total, also for the loss of five wickets. They then beat Linton Park of Kent, scoring 171 for 1 in reply to their opponents' 167 all out.

Their opponents in the Lord's final were Astwood Bank, a village just south of Redditch in Worcestershire. Coincidentally, in September 2003 when I was researching this book, Astwood Bank emerged as one of the two finalists once more – thirty-one years after they had competed in the very first of all. Back in 1972 they were captained by John Yoxall, a prolific batsman who had made over a thousand runs in eight consecutive seasons, and had a bowler called Joe Crompton who was described as a left-handed Denis Lillee. After beating four local rivals in the early rounds they made 209 for 7 against Hockley Heath in the fifth and won easily. In the sixth round they beat Swynnerton Park of Staffordshire by 124 for 4 against 101 all out, and then bowled out Horton House of Northamptonshire for 89, passing that total with only four wickets down.

In the quarter-finals they defeated Kimbolton of Huntingdonshire in similar style, bowling them out for 85 and winning by seven wickets. The semi-final against Collingham of Nottinghamshire was a much tighter game, with Collingham falling only three short of Astwood's 137 for 4, albeit for the loss of nine wickets.

Despite the nightmare derailment at Dawlish which kept six hundred Cornishmen from doing a Trelawney, that first final, on the second Saturday of September, attracted a crowd of three thousand. Astwood Bank made 165 for 8 in bad weather and fits and starts. Troon got off to a slow start in bad light. Twenty-three off the first twelve overs; fifty off sixteen; a hundred off twenty-three. And this thanks largely to skipper Terry Carter, who flayed the so-called left-handed Denis Lillee for eighteen off a single over and made 79 not out, hitting a winning six into the Tavern stand in only the thirty-fourth over.

A fine day's cricket, and yet there were some disquieting asides. For example, when Astwood Bank passed 100 the band of the Royal Green Jackets struck up a stirring march but the players, far from being elated, refused to play on until they desisted. I was reminded of Denis Compton's reaction on hearing how the players at Canterbury week had demanded the cessation of military music during play. Denis frowned thoughtfully. 'When I played at Canterbury, old boy,' he said to me, 'I used to try to bat in time to the music.' I felt the villagers should have done something similar with the Green Jackets. That gifted old England and Middlesex spinner, Ian Peebles, reporting in the *Observer*, remarked that 'immaculate dress and a high degree of professionalism had replaced the cow pat and the cow shot.'

Well, yes, one knew what he meant. Troon were, are, a lovely club. They exemplify a Cornish grit which I find very attractive, though outsiders are often unprepared for it. But they were a bit good. They had county players.

Years later I used to write occasional articles for the *Cricketer*, commissioned by Richard Hutton, son of Len, and son-in-law of Ben Brocklehurst. In 1996 I penned a piece about Troon at Richard's request and had a friendly note back saying 'thank you for your nice piece' but explaining

that he was going away for a month or so and was therefore passing it over to Ben Brocklehurst's PA who 'handles
the village competition'.

A day or so later I had a letter from the Brocklehurst
PA telling me that although Troon had won the championship three times in the early years, 'There have always been
adverse comments from several quarters that they are not a
true village.' In later years they had not been allowed to enter
because they had a paid professional on their books.

'The general feeling,' continued the letter, 'is that this
article might put off small village clubs from entering, indeed
those villages which are the backbone of the competition,
and which we are trying so hard to encourage.'

I know what they are getting at. I too have a vision of
squire and smith, parson and ploughman all competing equally
on a level playing field surrounded by rose-festooned cottages,
pubs, churches, manor-houses and spectating yokels. But life
is not like that even if it ever was, and the wishful thinking
is not fair on places like Troon. It's not Troon's fault that it's
in a depressed industrial area blighted by the demise of the
once mighty Holman's engineering works.

Anyway Troon stuffed the rosey-spectacled romantics by
winning the trophy three times in those early years. The litany
of finals is both instructive and evocative, not unlike one of
those Old Testament family trees in which a series of names
such as Obadiah and Nebuchadnezzar begat each other over
hundreds of years.

In 1972 Troon of Cornwall beat Astwood Bank of
Worcestershire, and the following year Troon beat Gowerton
of South Wales but only by 12 runs, and in 1974 Bomarsund
of Northumberland beat Collingham of Nottinghamshire at
Edgbaston after rain ruined play at Lord's. Then Gowerton

who had lost to Troon in 1973 beat Isleham of Cambridgeshire, and Troon came back the year after and defeated Sessay of North Yorkshire, and then Cookley of Worcester beat Lindal Moor of Cumbria, after which Toft of Cheshire lost to Linton Park of Kent and East Bierley of Yorkshire overcame Ynysgwern of Glamorgan and Marchwiel of Clwyd beat Longparish of Hampshire.

(Longparish are John Woodcock's team. Fancy them being beaten by the Welsh, but they came back in 1987 and beat Treeton Welfare of South Yorkshire by 76 runs. Treeton Welfare sounds like a funny sort of village.)

I like the noise of these results. It is the sound of an ancient England, except of course that on closer examination it is nothing of the sort. That Welsh win over the Hampshire men in 1980 was far from being a one-off. If you count the Cornish as Celts, which you surely must, then the Celtic fringe won the 'national' village cup on no fewer than eleven occasions. This translates, if my statistics are right, as more than a third of all victories. Moreover if you add in the half-dozen Celtic losing finalists you realise that over half of all the finals have been contested by Celts. More dispiriting still for a true Englishman is the fact that the only three-time winners are from Cornwall (Troon) and Glamorgan (St Fagan's). And there are some individual Celtic records as well. The highest score ever made in the competition was by a batsman named Wade who scored 239 not out for Goldsithney in an opening partnership of 373 against Ruan and Philleigh. That was an all-Cornish affair.

I'm always wary of statistics, whether it is batting averages or things like this, but if we are to believe in them at all it begins to look as if cricket at the grass-roots level in the British Isles is very far from being dominated by the English. Anyone who has spent summer days in Cornwall, Wales and

Scotland knows this to be true, and yet we stick to the belief that cricket is the most English of games. Is this perverse? It certainly isn't accurate today, if it ever was.

The results of the finals are only the tip of the iceberg. Back in 1973, for instance, Troon won the final scoring 176 for 3 against Gowerton's 164 for 5. But they could easily have gone out in the very first round to their old rivals Werrington, later the losing finalists in 1994. Werrington were only five runs short of Troon's 110 when their last man was bowled trying to hit a spectacular match-winning six in the final over.

Gowerton were back in 1975, when they won. It was their last time in the competition, because subsequently they were judged to have gone over the population limit and thus magically been transformed from a village to a town. By contrast, their opponents that year were a Cambridgeshire village with a green and a team which included three Houghton brothers and a brace each of Collens and Sheldricks. This was much more the sort of team and place that the founders of the competition had in mind when they invented it.

Unfortunately, however, you can't have a competition confined only to pretty villages which would look good in a picture postcard and in which, all the players are related to one another. It might be more fun if one could, but rules need to be precise, especially in this litigious age. Moreover the success of the competition has made people hyper-competitive in a way which, when I'm in seriously purist mode, I feel runs counter to the true spirit of the game. When I say that we live in a litigious age I was not being facetious. Ben Brocklehurst told me about a memorable moment when a village cricket club – or perhaps not a village cricket club – did indeed go to law.

'We are sensitive on the subject of villages,' he said, 'because we were taken to the High Court in Bristol by Usk C.C., whom we disqualified as not being a village. They'd been in the competition for nine years, having said that they were a village with a population of under three thousand. Due to the doubts raised by a village that were beaten by them by one run, we rang up an Usk secretary to check on the population, to be told that he wasn't sure but that his wife would know because she was Mayor two years ago. Further research showed that in the so-called village there were six banks and eleven pubs and that the football team was called Usk Town Football Club and that a large notice at the entrance to the village said "Welcome to the Historic Town of Usk".'

'We won the case.'

I know Usk, a pretty place in Monmouth with more hanging baskets of flowers than almost anywhere I know. I've had an enjoyable lunch in one of the eleven pubs. And I would never have described it as anything other than a small town. It is emphatically not a village. Yet I believe their team might well play what I think of as 'village cricket'. Their complaining opponents happened to be Werrington in Cornwall, which, as we have seen, began life as the Williams estate team and which barely qualifies even as a village, being more of a field in open countryside. Nevertheless they play in the first division of the Cornwall League and very nearly won it in 2003. They have also been in a Lord's final. When it comes to cricket I'm sure you could argue that their game is less 'villageish' than Usk's.

There is controversy on the field of play as well as off it.

Rule 16 of the competition specifies that 'The highest standards and best spirit of the game, as specified in the 'Preamble to the Laws of Cricket', must be observed both

on and off the field. In the unlikely event of any team failing to uphold these standards, the committee reserves the
right to disqualify them.'

Oh dear, the path to hell is strewn with good intentions
or whatever the saying is. Tim Brocklehurst's job, as the principal arbiter of fair play, spirit of the game, stiff-upper-lip-
manship and straight-battery, was often fraught. Take this, for
example, which arrived on his desk in May 2003. It was from
the chairman of Hurstbourne Priors Cricket Club, who had
been captaining his team in round two of the cup's North
Hampshire Region against Dogmersfield. His name was Page.
Hurstbourne Priors won the toss and elected to bat. They
were all out for 150 and the record shows that Dogmersfield
made 150 for six; which meant they won by dint of losing
fewer wickets. This was what the Hurstbourne Priors skipper wrote. His first paragraph, under the heading 'Highlight',
ran as follows:

The match ended in controversial circumstances. With
Dogmersfield needing 3 from the last ball to win out-
right or 2 to tie the game (but winning on fewer
wickets lost). HPCC held them to one run, narrowly
missing a run-out as the wicketkeeper took off the bails
at the striker's end. Believing the ball to be dead at this
point the HPCC players, including the wicketkeeper
still with the ball, formed a celebration huddle on the
square. Without the wicketkeeper in attendance at the
stumps, the batsmen then decided to run, under encour-
agement from team-mates in the pavilion, and to the
amazement of the HPCC team, were awarded the match.

Then, under 'Comment', the captain wrote:

Although extremely disappointed HPCC did not challenge the decision as we had arrived without an umpire and agreed beforehand to two Dogmersfield officials to adjudicate. However we are still unconvinced as to the legality of the action. If it was legal then we were either grossly naïve, or they were guilty of unsporting behaviour. Perhaps we could have the *Cricketer* view – it would certainly make the result easier to swallow, especially as we have yet to win a single fixture in the competition.

Tough one. I must say all my sympathies are with Hurstbourne Priors, though I think their captain's 'or' is misplaced. It seems to me that their 'gross naïvety' and Dogmersfield's 'unsporting behaviour' were not alternatives but necessary adjuncts. The latter wouldn't have been possible without the former. Mr Page sounds a nice chap, though. At the end of his note he scribbled, in handwriting, 'It was otherwise a fine game of cricket.' I'm afraid Tim Brocklehurst did what I suppose he had to, which was judge that the umpire's decision was final. I, on the other hand, would have disqualified Dogmersfield for not behaving 'in the best spirit of the game'. In my book they should have been disqualified under Rule 16 even though they were technically within their rights.

I might have understood if money had been at stake, but I've never got the hang of people who are happy winning games such as this by any means. Money has always been a challenge for the Village Cup. Some villages obviously have it and others don't, but there is no way in which the rules can take account of this. There have been occasions when 'village' sides drawn against opponents in a far corner of the

Kingdom have chartered an aeroplane to make the journey – they haven't always been rewarded with a win. Such extravagance would be far beyond the wildest dreams of other villages. Wealth must have an effect on playing standards, mustn't it? But how can you penalise rich villages and reward poor ones? And should you even try? This is village cricket, not social engineering.

It costs money to organise and it costs money to provide the prizes. The *Cricketer* never had huge resources of its own and relied on outside sponsorship whenever possible. Haig's whisky sponsored the first six years, Whitbread's the brewers also did six and Norsk Hydro did four. Rothmans, the cigarette people, the Alliance and Leicester, and Wadworth 6X did three apiece. In between these the *Cricketer* itself had, on several occasions, to step into the breach. For a monthly magazine with modest sales this was a tall order.

Trying to attract a sponsor for 2003 – unsuccessfully – the *Cricketer* costed the package at £120,000. 'This is a championship,' claimed the magazine to potential sponsors, 'that enables those at the grass roots of the game to be recognised both regionally and nationally. It fosters the traditions of rural Britain while providing a showcase for the Spirit of Cricket. In doing so, it touches the hearts and imagination of everyone British.'

Quite so, but no one bit.

Worse still, the *Cricketer* itself expired. A deal with the Getty-owned *Wisden Cricket Monthly* was billed as a merger but looked far more like a take-over. At the end of August I called Paula Bachelor, the immensely hard-working organiser of the competition, to find that the last edition of the magazine had gone to bed and the last member of the editorial staff had cleared his desk, packed his bag, hung up his pads and gone home. The beautiful converted Kentish oast-house sounded an empty and disconsolate place.

Nevertheless the 2003 tournament went ahead as planned. There were nearer five hundred entrants than the original eight hundred: fewer clubs, stricter application of rules on population and professionalism, opposition from local leagues. All the same over five hundred villages represents a formidable achievement in terms of organisation and motivation, and the list of entries still reads like a poem by Thomas Hardy or Ted Hughes. A celebration of countryside, a paean to place.

> Gargunnock and Newton Hill, Ross County and Kintore
> Fochabers, Doune, Luncarty, Breadalbane
> Warkworth, Chatton, Cowpen Bewley, Bomarsund
> Belsay and Mitford, Boosbeck and Burnhope
> Middleton Tyas, Chop Gate, Aldbrough St John, Harome
> Sessay and Bishop Thornton, Burton Leonard, Bolton Percy
> Oulton and Hooton Pagnell, Oughtibridge and Wadworth
> Bramhope and Carlton, Bardsey and Addingham
> Threlkeld and Silverdale, Chipping and Sedgwick
> Charnock Richard and Grimsagh, Wrea Green and Mawdsley and Caldy
> Pontblyddyn, Pott Shrigley, Llanrhaeadr, Styal, Mere
> Papplewick and Lindby, Plumtree, Skellingthorpe
> Draycott and Hanbury, Condover, Quatt
> Thorpe Arnold, Gracedieu Park
> Brockhampton, Astwood Bank, Chaddesley, Cookley, Garnons

Rushton and Gretton, Kislington Temperance and
Byfield

Llangwm, Drefach and Bronwydd Arms

Tondu, Llanarth, Miskin Manor and Ynystawe

Hillesley and Dumbleton, Birdlip and Brimpsfield,
Bredon and Fairford, Stone

Chalgrove, Cropredey and Britwell Salome, Kingston
Bagpuize and Buscot Park

Hambleden, Dinton and Kimble, Great Horwood and
Great Hampden

North Mymms and Botany Bay

Waresley and Wormley and Bayford

Havering-Atte-Bower, Stock, Great Burstead, Audley
End

Barrington, Bluntisham, Fordham and Swardeston

Fonthill and Potterne, Redlynch and Hale,

Hinton Blewitt, Brompton Ralph, Chew Magna and
Fitzhead

Perranworthal, Menheniot, Roche and Grampound
Road

Feniton, Clyst Hydon, Plymtree, Clyst St George

Easton and Martyr Worthy, Curdrige and Amport,
Hurstbourne Priors

Capel and Newdigate, Shere and Badshot Lea

Goodwood and Outwood, Findon and Waldron, Harting
and Ditchling, Herstmonceux

Underriver, Highways at Platt, High Halstow and Linton
Park.

These are just a few of the 2003 contestants, and I admit
that some of these lines scan better than others and none of
them rhyme. You couldn't therefore describe it as verse, but

dull would he be of soul who wouldn't concede that it's poetry of a sort.

The 2003 contest resulted in a final between two stalwarts of the championship scene. These were Astwood Bank of Worcestershire, who had been blown away by Cornish Troon in the very first year of the competition, and the reigning champions, Shipton-under-Wychwood of Oxfordshire, who had defeated Elvaston of Derbyshire by five wickets the previous year.

'Bit of a local Derby,' remarked Mike Yapp, chairman of Astwood Bank, who was predicting six hundred Worcestershire supporters. 'We're only about forty miles apart.' Mike was an environmental health inspector and a keen former player who had joined the club in 1977.

Despite their geographical proximity the clubs had very different backgrounds. Shipton were classic country-house-converts. Theirs is a fine ground with a distinctive lych-gate leading on to it, an original wooden pavilion and a back-drop of enormous English trees. It was laid out as a private ground for the Jacobean Shipton Court, but a village club was formed in 1933 and immediately after the Second World War they were able to purchase the freehold, playing happily on their own turf ever since.

Their chairman, Geoff Miles, a civil engineer, Shipton born and bred and a former player like his opposite number, said that in his view the strength of village cricket in the Village Cup was a matter of pockets, and the Midland area which included both the 2003 finalists was one of the centres of excellence. In fact, he said, looking mildly embarassed, it was almost more difficult to get out of Oxfordshire than to win the 'national' rounds. Old sparring partners such as Kingston Bagpuize and Aston Rowant were notoriously tough nuts to crack. Shipton were traditionally a farmers' team who always suspended their fixtures during harvest time.

Astwood Bank, on the other hand, came from an industrial base and have been playing far longer than their Oxfordshire neighbours – certainly since 1860, possibly since 1843. The village was originally a centre of the needle-making trade. The original club was formed by four local needle-making companies and played its first games against other companies, joining the *Four Shires Advertiser* League in 1890. Although the ground was, and is, in Warwickshire, the village itself is in Worcestershire, and it is in the Worcestershire League that the club has played most of its cricket since the formation of the league in 1973.

I sat on one of the long tables in the Long Room and watched the players walk out. There was only one other spectator in the room, an elderly chap in a rhubarb and custard, bacon and egg, MCC tie. The spectators outside were nearly all in the Mound and Tavern stands, because the wicket was on the edge of that side of the square. The Warner stand and the Grand Stand were too far away for a spectator to be able to see more than white-flannelled matchstick men flickering to and fro in the distance. The boundary rope on that side of Lord's was miles from the seating.

I'm never too certain about crowd estimates. Someone said later that there were a couple of thousand in the ground. There were certainly more than I've seen for many Middlesex county matches, especially in mid-week, and they were much more vociferous. It felt more like the Oval than staid, even stuffy old Lord's.

Sitting there in that beautiful room with its ancient bats and balls and the portraits of all manner of different cricketers from John Nyren – died 1837 – to Keith Miller –

happily still with us at the time of writing I reflected on the half-century of cricket I myself had already seen at cricket's HQ and thought of the great cricketers I had seen performing on the immaculate turf. I think my very first game began with Brian Statham bowling at a Middlesex side that included Edrich and Compton. Now here I was watching village cricketers from Oxfordshire and Worcestershire. What must they be feeling as they walked through that historic room through which so many giants of the game had paced over a hundred years and more? What must I be feeling as I watched with the only other Long Room spectator?

Truth be told, my main thought was that they looked much like any other fielding team and any other pair of opening batsmen. They certainly looked nothing like as eccentric as Squire Osbaldeston or the Revd Lord Frederic Beauclerk would have appeared when they fought out their single-wicket duels. Or even Prebendary Wickham of Martock when he turned out for Somerset against Middlesex. Astwood Bank wore crisp whites and green baseball caps. Jason Constable and Steve Bates, the Shipton openers, were armoured like gladiators, walking stiffly, their faces almost obscured by the grilles of their helmets.

Astwood Bank had elected to bowl because they were nervous of nerves. You would expect a journeyman village cricketer to be jittery when performing here, but Shipton had been the year before and might be expected to have conquered nerves. Not so Astwood Bank, who were last at Lord's over thirty years ago, when John Robinson, father of today's captain Alex Robinson, was playing for the team. The club has also had a strong family tradition. In the thirties three fathers and their sons played in the same side. Some of the present team had family links going right back to 1900.

The Worcester men's fear of nerves seemed justified, for Bowes's first two balls were far too short and gentle-paced and Jason Constable swung across the line and punched them both for pugnacious boundaries around mid-wicket. The first over went for nine, the second for eight.

I moved from the Victorian stateliness of the Long Room to the plate-glass, state-of-the-art press centre high above the middle of the Compton and Edrich stands at the Nursery End and watched as Constable and Bates put on 63 for the first wicket. Then Astwood Bank's nerves must have settled or maybe their first-change bowlers, Summers and Sealey, were better than the opening pair. In any event 63 for no wicket became 93 for 5. Summers' nine overs cost a niggardly eleven runs and Sealey's twenty-two, though he got three wickets to his colleague's one.

This seemed to represent a decisive swing in Astwood Bank's favour. Watching from my space-age eyrie I had a tremendous bird's-eye view of the play, but the players seemed such a long way below and the whole area so insulated from sound outside that it was like watching a silent movie or TV with the sound turned off. After drinks, half-way through the innings there was a bit of a flurry, but the innings closed on 149.

Lord's is a fascinating combination of ancient and modern, and on this occasion it was good to see that the villagers were enjoying all the modernities. Every time a new bats-man came in his name was announced over the Tannoy and flashed up on the big screen. And not just his name but his 'nickname'. I knew that nicknames were defining features of cricketing dressing-rooms at all levels, but I had never before seen them so much an ingredient in the potted biographies of all the players. Thus for Shipton: Paul Hemming, nickname 'Hemmo', age 39, job title Self-employed Courier Driver; followed by Steve 'Bambi' Bates, a 26-year-old Civil Servant; Stewart 'Gilly' Gillet, 33, Information Services Manager; Jason 'Shrek' Constable, 30, Environmental Officer. Then there was a Curriculum Administrator called Yoda; Luigi, the IT engineer; 'Duffo', the Cheltenham Town footballer; 'Pants', the Company Proprietor; 'Sniper', the Company Director; 'Orb', the Systems Manager; 'Lambo', the Student; 'Windy', the Distribution Manager; 'Brainer', the Sports Field Assistant Groundsman; and 'Chipmunk', the Student. Astwood Bank were Spud; JJ (Jock Junior); Grandad – Ian Bowes, who once played for Aston Unity, the club immortalised by the great novelist J.L. Carr in *The First Saturday in May*; Boyo or Badger; Mule; Clarky or Clackers; Del-Boy or AC; Gimp; Gonk or Vernon; Bevo; Coco the Clown and Pest; Wonker or Gibbon; Robbo; Digby and Flapper; Slops; Pilot Light and Twigger.

During the lunch interval I had a beer with Mike Yapp, Astwood Bank's chairman. He seemed quietly confident, that 149 was a total well within his side's grasp. To judge from earlier finals it looked as if a winning total was somewhere between about 190 and 250, and I was inclined to agree with Mike that 149 wasn't going to present too much of a problem. On the other hand the immediate precedents weren't so encouraging. In the previous year Shipton had bowled out Elvaston of Derbyshire, the 2000 winners, for just 122. Meanwhile Astwood Bank had exceeded 200 in every round of the Worcester, Hereford and Powys Championship. Well, it's a funny old game and Mike Yapp said his was a strong side. It was the first time since the late eighties that they had entered the competition, and they wouldn't have done so if they didn't rate their chances.

'Slops' Sealey, a professional musician, and 'Del Boy' Clayton, a production manager, put on 31 for the first wicket, which was a sound start. On the other hand it was only half the score of the Shipton openers and it was scored slowly. From the comfort of the Brocklehursts' box in the Tavern Stand it looked as if it was, as they had feared, a failure of nerve. After getting bogged down the Worcester men tried to slog their way out of trouble. On the other side of the Thames Andrew 'Freddie' Flintoff was demonstrating how to change a game by powerful hitting when he thumped an extraordinary 95 for England against South Africa. To do that succesfully in any level of cricket, however, you need a technique and application which, on the day at least, the Astwood Bank players didn't have. After only 32.5 of their allotted 40 overs their innings fizzled out for a measley 79, leaving Shipton-under-Wychwood the victors by 67.

It was a bit of an anticlimax, though the supporters of both sides gathered cheerily enough under the pavilion for presentations by the MCC secretary Roger Knight, and Knight made all the right noises about the virtues of village cricket. Perhaps I felt a certain piquancy chatting to Ben Brocklehurst in the final moments of play, for this was the last time the competition's final would be held under the aegis of his magazine. He had been proprietor of the *Cricketer* since 1971 but it had now published its last independent edition after a history which began with the great P.F. 'Plum' Warner in 1921. Those nicknames again. The Village Cup had been Ben's baby and now it was going to become a Getty project. For all the generosity of Paul Getty's cricket legacy you couldn't help feeling a little sad. Paula Bachelor, who as Tim Brocklehurst's assistant had organised this year's competition, had resigned and was off to try her hand at independent consultancy. The magazine's editorial offices would no longer be in that beautiful Kentish oast-house but in an office in London somewhere near the A40.

I felt that an era in which the village competition had been presided over by a man who was at heart a village cricketer himself was passing. I could see that in future the cup might be bigger and better and more financially healthy, but I wasn't entirely sure that I felt that was what village cricket required. But then although I could see that for the twenty-two players who performed that day a Lord's final was a high spot in an otherwise ordinary cricketing life, I wasn't entirely sure either that village cricket belonged at Lord's, on such a grand and famous stage. Part of me could see the romantic allure of a village final on the best-known ground in the world but another part of me felt that village cricket belonged in one place alone.

That part of me believed in a slope more steep than that at Lord's, in surrounding trees and hills and perhaps a stream, cottages, a pub and an ancient church. I'd draw the line at cow-pats and sheep droppings, but I'd approve a sporting surface and home advantage for those who understood the vicissitudes of the local wicket. St John's Wood may be the home of cricket, but I'm not convinced that it's the true home of the most English form of cricket.

That, surely, can only be the village green.

6

Stockbroker Surrey, Centenary Essex

If my theories are correct then the nearer one gets to London and the stockbroker belt the further one gets from the essence of traditional village cricket. On the other hand there is a part of me that says that the spirit of cricket is so strong that it transcends the vicissitudes of wealth, trendiness, metropolitanism and everything that goes with living within or within coughing distance of the tarmac necklace of the M25.

The club president believes that his Berkshire field is 'a lovely cricket ground – 900-year-old church on boundary edge, sixes into the Thames. Kept going by my Showbiz Day. Big crowd, lots of shows, cricketers too.'

It is President Parkinson speaking and by a happy coincidence the church just over the boundary fence is dedicated to St Michael. Sacrilege to suggest that there is anything particularly saintly about Mike Parkinson, except that in the matter of the Maidenhead and Bray Cricket Club he could reasonably claim to be its saviour. It might be overstating the case to say that it would have died without him, but not much. The brand new covers, the smart sight-screens, the immaculate wickets prepared by a salaried groundsman, the hundred or so young cricketers who attend nets every week . . . is all this down to Saint Mike?

Well not entirely, but the influence of this quintessential son of the northern soil, the Barnsley boy with the dyspeptic disapproval of fancy-hat southerners, on this opulent Home Counties patch of turf has been disproportionate and unexpected. Every year President Parky stages a razzmatazz showbiz fund-raising event with stars and celebrities of every description.

Bray is the soft underbelly of affluent England. Literally so, for its most famous landmark apart, perhaps, from the church and the cricket ground is the Waterside Restaurant of Michael Roux. Here, along the narrow lane leading to the River Thames, the Jaguars and the Bentleys and the stretched Mercedes glide in and out of valet parking and the *menu gastronomique* is £33.50. Nearer the village centre the Fat Duck offers a set lunch for £25.75, starting with a fricassee of cockerels' kidneys and *girolles*. And overlooking the ground itself, the eighteenth-century Chauntry House is a fifteen-room hotel whose restaurant offers risotto with lobster in a champagne and saffron mousseline as well as 'jus', 'papillotte' and 'cinnamon sabayon'. It's all a far cry from the old-fashioned sandwiches prepared by the club's redoubtable tea lady, Mrs Bennett.

Mrs Bennett retired from tea-making not long ago but returned to the colours after the club's only spectator, Cyril Hollis, resigned in sympathy. Cyril went because in 2001 there was a dramatic change in club policy. The year before large sums of money had been spent on the services of the former Middlesex and England spin bowler, John Emburey. Cyril evidently enjoyed watching Emburey and another hired hand, a Pakistani.

President Parkinson paid warm tribute to Emburey who, he said, 'did a remarkable job, even persuading them to indulge in warm-up exercises, nets and other hitherto alien practices such as walking on to the field as a purposeful unit instead of straggling on looking like the remnants of the London Marathon.'

At the end of the 2000 season, however, Emburey was asked back to Middlesex and the Maidenhead and Bray club had to decide whether to find a replacement or to do with-out. President Parky and the club chairman, Jamie Sears, who between them seem to take most of the important decisions, settled down for a chat and agreed to take a radically differ-ent approach. Instead of buying in expensive ready-manufactured talent they decided to save money and spend it on nurturing local youngsters.

What had happened at Bray was a mirror-image of the picture elsewhere and especially in county cricket. The pool of home-grown players was drying up and instead of trying to plug the dyke the remedy was the quick but expensive fix of bringing in what Parkinson described as a 'constant flow of young Australians, Pakistanis, South Africans and Kiwis, whose skills and attitudes were honed by a system we could only envy'.

The situation was made worse because one or two superior players could change a plain team into a good one and win matches without any undue exertion from the bulk of the players. The idea, or one of them, was that the example of a superior professional player should spur on the others. Sometimes this happened. Jamie Cox's motivation of a previously ordinary Somerset side into a cup-winning outfit who came second in the championship was a case in point. The Tasmanian skipper inspired the rest of the team. Just as often, though, the reverse happened, as at Essex, where the better their Queensland import Stuart Law played, the worse the English members of the team seemed to perform. Importing highly paid outsiders bought questionable benefits which hardly anyone could afford.

'In common with county cricket,' said Parkinson, 'we were paying with money we hadn't earned. In other words we had to beg, borrow and steal to finance our ambitions. Subscriptions from our players just about cover the cost of the balls we use during a season.

'This is the economic reality of local cricket. What is more, and most importantly, we have found over the last decade or so more and more children coming to the club for coaching.

'Partly this is due to the dedication of caring men, but mainly it is because in many areas clubs have replaced schools as the nurseries for young cricketers. So we decided to concentrate on youth and do away with expensive hired help.'

This grass-roots policy was all very well – admirable in fact – but as the president explained, 'This inevitably meant the first team going into free-fall.'

This was certainly happening on the September Saturday when I went to Bray. The home side batted first against a strongish Lensbury side from Thamseside Teddington and wickets fell fast and often.

Before play began, however, I walked across to the church, one of whose incumbents was, in his day, as famous as Michel Roux or even Michael Parkinson. This was the Vicar of Bray, about whom the English folk song was written. My Brewer's *Dictionary of Phrase and Fable* says that he was 'semi-legendary' but was most probably based on Samuel Alleyne who, according to one source, 'lived in the reigns of Henry VIII, Edward VI, Mary, and Elizabeth. In the first two reigns he was Protestant, in Mary's reign he turned Papist, and in the next reign recanted – being resolved, whoever was king, to die Vicar of Bray.'

Or, as the words of the song put it,

> This is law I will maintain
> Until my dying day, Sir
> That whatsoever king shall reign,
> I'll still be the Vicar of Bray, Sir.

Confusion arises from the actual words which Brewer says were written in 'Restoration times' by an officer in Colonel Fuller's regiment. The song-sheets on sale in the Parish church say that the tune is seventeenth century and the words eighteenth. As the last verse refers to 'Th'illustrious house of Hanover' it must have been written at least a quarter of a century later.

From a brief study of the list of vicars on the church wall my guess is that the Vicar in the song is Hezekiah Woodward who was vicar from 1650 to 1709 and would therefore have been appointed under Cromwell and served under Charles II, James II, William and Mary, and Anne. You would have to have been quite a successful trimmer to have pulled off that feat, and so Hezekiah is my man even though conventional wisdom prefers Samuel Alleyne.

There wasn't much evidence of a connection between Church and cricket though I was intrigued to see that the seventeenth-century Archbishop of Canterbury, William Laud, left 'ten pounds yearly for two years in three for putting out a poor Boy Apprentice (boy to be chosen on 7th October)' but there's nothing to suggest that such a boy ever became a young professional cricketer. In fact, there was a long period when the Church owned the cricket field. There are still cricketers in Bray who remember that on a Sunday play was never allowed to start until the church bells signalled the end of mattins and no matter what the state of the game play was required to cease the instant the same bell tolled to summon the faithful for evensong.

Back in the pavilion bar President Parkinson, casual in a Boss top and with infant grandchildren in attendance, bought me a pint but stuck to water himself. He first saw the ground in 1970 when he came to represent the Second Eleven of a nearby picturesque Thameside village. It was love at first sight and a couple of years later he bought the riverine house there which has been his home ever since.

Further south and also just beyond the tarmac necklace of the M25 lies Coldharbour, tucked away at the foot of Leith Hill, east of Dorking. This is pretty country, but it's stock-broker belt too.

Ralph Vaughan Williams, Josiah Wedgwood and Charles Darwin all once lived in Coldharbour. *The Lark Ascending,*

Staffordshire pottery and *The Origin of Species*. Not a bad treble for a small Surrey village snuggled in the North Downs. Darwin was Wedgwood's grandson. Bill Travers, the actor, who was married to Virginia McKenna and starred with her in the film *Born Free*, was buried in the churchyard.

For all this esoteric information I am indebted to my man in Coldharbour, Jeffrey Rayner. Jeffrey has a PR company which deals in exotic foreign parts and I have been undertaking 'Raynertours' ever since he sent me to Calabria in the early seventies. When he heard that I was writing about village cricket he immediately told me that I must write about his local village ground because it was, in a literal sense, the most elevated in southern England.

It is indeed high on the hillside, surrounded by trees, though a view has been cut through the woods so that on a clear day you can see the main runway of Gatwick airport in the plain below. The ground is also small, so that there are special rules. In order to score a six the ball must actually clear the perimeter fence. Hitting it, even on the full, is not good enough and only counts four. It is surrounded by trees and undergrowth, some of which seemed on my visit to have put the heavy roller out of action.

Jeffrey is not a player but he is an enthusiastic spectator and a Lord's Taverner no less. That evening the author Leslie Thomas and his wife Diana were coming to stay and they were all heading off for a musical evening at Richard Stilgoe's place. The Thomases are old friends of Jeffrey's as well as being cricket enthusiasts in their own right.

When I arrived at Jeffrey's he and some friends were in the garden shooting clay pigeons. After that we went down to the pub for just the one, and he then prepared a salad lunch with delicious new potatoes fresh from the garden. To drink I had just the other, so that by the time we drove up to the ground I was feeling rather soporific and Sunday afternoonish on one of the few sunny days in that sodden June. My mild sleepiness was enhanced by the fact that the opposition were a local wandering side named Mogador. This immediately made me think of Mogadon although it is actually the name of a village just outside Reigate and the wandering Mogador's cricket did not seem particularly somnambulist.

'Give it some air, Major,' shouted one of the younger fielders as Mogador's senior citizen trundled in off what the heckling outfielder described as 'your long run'. Another man in the outfield had a pint mug of beer strategically positioned just off the field of play. His sips after each ball suggested a lack of urgency which was infectious. In the end, and after I had left, stumps were drawn after forty-six overs of Mogador which yielded 265 for 9 and forty-two of Coldharbour which produced 251 for 8. This was high scoring, though the local journalist and enthusiastic cricketer Tony Dawe told me that the club record was 436, which the home side scored in an all-day match in 1995 against Newdigate who rather unwisely agreed to fifty overs apiece. Dawe also remembered a game when Coldharbour declared at 4.20 p.m. after less than two hours' batting. They had reached 262 for 3 and a beefy young American called Michael Kornrumpf who later captained Dorking Rugby Club was on 150 not out.

For the first fifty odd years of its existence the Coldharbour club played on a ground which was described by the former England captain, Arthur (A.E.R.) Gilligan as the smallest in England. It was only fifty-eight yards long and thirty-five wide – even smaller than the present field, which I'm afraid I did not measure.

Gilligan came down in 1936 to report on a game with the neighbouring village of Abinger for a now defunct publication called the *Daily Chronicle*. He described how the ground was bisected by the road round Leith Hill which was only twenty-five yards from the wicket. One of the umpires, a man called Thornden, told him that he risked his life for village cricket because when he stood at square leg he 'had to keep one eye on the traffic and the other on the game'.

This was not the only hazard. There was a potential cow-pat situation and before play that morning the Coldharbour men removed the posts and chains guarding the green and drove off a herd of cows browsing peacefully round it. The wicket itself was 'like a quagmire' at one end and quite dry at the other. Runs consequently were scored mainly in singles and on this occasion Coldharbour only made 44 but still managed to win by 21 runs. There were exceptions to this singles-only convention. A partnership of two Coldharbour gardeners, Smith and Comber, who came together at the fall of the first wicket, 'ran a five for a glorious hit down the hill'. Abinger got six for a lost ball after the batsmen had run four. The ball remained lost despite all the efforts of five fielders and two dogs.

The field could by no stretch of the imagination be described as even remotely flat or even. Indeed Gilligan wrote: 'The Coldharbour team boast that they generally win at home – chiefly because of this slope. For when the ball is hit down it, the batsman cannot see what has happened and many an unwary visitor has been run out. The Abinger team, who arrived by lorry, brought with them several scouts who were posted on the hill on the north side, and shouted advice to their batsmen when to run and when not to run.'

After close of play Gilligan suffered an apparently familiar experience.

'The Coldharbour team came to my assistance and pushed my car – which had settled firmly in the boggy ground – back on to the road with cries of "We are useful all-rounders at every game".'

The Second World War finally put paid to this eccentric playing field. Tony Dawe explained that the ground became overgrown and the pipes carrying water from the springs on the hillside burst and the road finally became so busy that it really was a serious threat to the life of the square-leg umpire.

Immediately after the war the club played a few games on a ground at the Pigott-Browns' estate at Broome Hall, between Coldharbour and Otley, but the village understandably wanted its own place. Two possible sites were rejected because they were too bleak or remote, but third time proved lucky and they moved on to the present patch by the path up to Leith Tower, two hundred feet higher than their previous ground and half a mile from the pub. A few holes were cut in the surrounding woodland so that players and spectators could see out. Some holes in the playing surface were plugged and the 'pavilion' – previously a stores shed at Kenley aerodrome – was brought in on a lorry. There was no running water and only bottled gas.

The star of this post-war period has been Reg Comber who, when I was there, was still living within a few minutes' walk of the Plough and who played for Coldharbour for more than fifty years. To celebrate his Golden Jubilee in 1991 the club hired the Oval. 'It was a great day,' recalled Reg a decade or so later. 'All I'd wanted was to play a game against the captains of all the local clubs I'd played against during my time with the club. But they hired the Oval and I said that it would be good if as many of us as possible could play so we had a mix-up among ourselves.' Reg batted at four for the Captain's Eleven against the President's and was out caught for eight, though the number of runs was the least of his or anyone else's concerns. There was also a grand dinner that year with Alec Bedser as the guest of honour.

Reg's family were practically all Coldharbour players, indeed his Comber uncle was one of the two gardeners who ran the famous five while his grandfather, Jim Groomridge, captained the team for many years and also played in 'Gilligan's match'. As a small boy Reg always used to form up at matches bringing his kit with him and hoping that Coldharbour would be a man short and he'd be summoned to make up the numbers. This finally happened in 1941 and he responded effectively enough to begin to win a place on merit.

The robust programme notes for the jubilee game at the Oval state that 'Reg has batted at 1–11, fielded in every position possible and bowled wicked spinners . . . he has been a past skipper and has prepared many a track up the hill.' His hobbies were listed as 'Cricket, beer, whiskey, food – not necessarily in that order!' and his ambitions as 'To play cricket for Coldharbour for another fifty years'. They were, of course, those sort of notes. Tony Dawe, who wrote them, listed his own nickname as 'Ten Dinners' and said that his ambition was 'To eat up his nickname'.

Dawe has written of Reg Comber that 'he looks the perfect village cricketer.'

His rotund figure and round weather-beaten face suggest the years of leaning on the pavilion gate discussing the abilities and shortcomings of generations of locals. But in fifty years of playing for Coldharbour village cricket club, his style has belied that appearance. He can bat beautifully and at the height of his career people would come and watch Coldharbour to see Comber bat. He struck the ball sweetly but also perfected those deflections which earn an easy four on the small Coldharbour pitch. On one occasion on Brockham Green in the early 1970s, he received a bollocking from an old gent as he left the pitch after an uncharacteristic duck. 'I walked two mile to see you and you get nowt, you duffer,' shouted the irascible spectator.

Comber was captain of Coldharbour in the sixties which involved leading from in front as a batsman (at least a dozen centuries) and from behind the stumps as wicketkeeper. Almost more importantly it also involved opening up the pavilion, making sure the tea was served and, as Tony Dawe observed, 'that least popular of jobs' – emptying the ladies' loo.

By the time I got to Coldharbour Reg Comber was in blameless retirement at home hard by the Plough, looking back on his prime with pleasure and at the present with a beady scepticism. 'It was much more fun in those days,' he said, 'but it's what you make of it. The trouble with the leagues is that it's become so important not to lose so you get two sides going out there and battling for a draw. Well that's not village cricket.'

He certainly makes the old days sound entertaining: the games against the Jolly Rogers who were the Blackheath Rugby Club in disguise; the time the ball went for four off Jack's elbow; and the other game when one chap got all nine wickets before another bowler chipped in with just the one and the one who took the nine wouldn't speak to the one who got the one for weeks afterwards on account of the fact that he'd prevented him going into the record book as the taker of all ten wickets.

Which, come to think of it, sounds as serious as anything that the modern leagues produce and confirms the sense that even at Coldharbour times don't change as much as the old stagers think they do. Nothing is ever as much fun as it was, and even in Coldharbour times change. In 2000 Alec Stewart came with a celebrity team including Ben Hollioake and Will Carling, scored a quick-fire century, helped raise £10,000 for the village church and said it was the best-supported game of that kind he'd ever played in. Not quite like Gilligan's game in 1936 when the teams managed only 67 between them.

Fun all the same. I don't suppose Wedgwood, Darwin or even Vaughan Williams played cricket. Wedgwood and Darwin would have made a formidable opening pair with Vaughan Williams as first change and Reg Comber standing up behind the stumps, Arthur Gilligan to write the match report and Jeffrey Rayner to provide lunch. Evening recital by Stilgoe and his partner Peter Skellern. Tall tales from Leslie Thomas. All three local Lord's Taverners were there in real life at Stilgoe's charity event that evening.

Perfect end to a perfect day.

Great Bentley plays its cricket on the second largest village green in Essex. Not many people know this. Great Bentley Green is forty-five acres compared to Woodside Green in Great and Little Hallingbury, which is over sixty-two acres, though Great Bentley champions maintain that Woodside is more of a common than a green in the strict meaning of the act.

Great Bentley Green goes back to Saxon times and could

be as old as 1500 years. Open common land in Essex started to be enclosed in the fourteenth and fifteenth centuries, but Great Bentley Green escaped until during a spate of enclosures in 1812 it came under threat. The villagers were incensed and elected one of their number, a man called Peter Thompson, to act as their spokesman and petition Parliament on their behalf. As a result King George IV signed a proclamation to the effect that the Green should remain unenclosed for all time 'to be used for the grazing of cattle and the sport and recreation of the villagers'.

The village lies far out beyond Colchester, *en route* to Clacton-on-Sea, in that attractive part of the county which outsiders, thinking only of suburban Essex and 'Essex girls', seldom comprehend.

Tim Jordan, a cricketing villager of more than twenty years' standing, says that the village club 'is a very old and interesting club and we play cricket in a wonderful setting'. This, he thinks, is best appreciated 'on a warm summer's evening with cricket being played and the sun going down over the Hall Farm and the Red Lion and behind it the church tower'.

There is a local school of thought which believes cricket has been played there for more than 250 years. Certainly the village is recorded as playing against the Gentlemen of Essex for a barrel of beer in 1790, and for a decade in the early 1800s they even participated in an early league, drawing players from a wide area. Eventually, however, it was decided that this was too stressful and competitive and Great Bentley reverted to 'friendly' cricket with players drawn from within the community.

The club has never gained full control over its ground and even in modern times was refused permission to put a rope round the wicket as this could be construed as the illegal fencing of common land.

The most extraordinary match played by Great Bentley, indeed one of the oddest in the annals of village cricket, must be that between them and the Suffolk village of Bures to the north-east, just south of Sudbury. In 1845 these two rivals met for a match in Bures. Great Bentley batted first and lost four quick wickets, the batsmen falling for 13, 11, 8 and 0.

The Great Bentley opener, N. Bromley, was then joined by W. Cant. These two put the Bures attack to the sword, with Bromley eventually falling for 83. Cant went on to 165 not out and the game finished with Great Bentley on 301 for 9 when the visitors had to call it a day and make their way home. For some unfathomable reason they promised to return to finish the match but only in a hundred years' time.

The Second World War was a contributory factor in preventing this hundred-year return and it was not until 22 June 1957 that Great Bentley came back, wearing top hats and completing their journey in a vintage harvest wagon. As soon as they arrived Mick Allington, the Bentley captain, declared his side's innings closed and put Bures in to bat. The umpires were in smocks, the scorers recorded notches, the bowling was underarm and each over was four balls.

The score-board certainly ticked over and the innings was eventful from the very first. The second ball was a wide and the fourth went for a six. Harry Morton made 50 in 41 minutes and after he was caught at point an eighteen-year-old bakery student called Dennis Hume hit 124 in 111 minutes including a six and sixteen fours. The Bures score was 199 after just an hour and a half, and when they reached 300 there were only five wickets down and the match looked dead and buried. This game was not over, however, for Phil Nevard of Bentley then did the hat-trick, leaving the home side a run short with just two wickets in hand. Finally Maurice Cansdale of Bures hit the last ball of the hat-trick over for four and the home side had triumphed by two wickets. They then batted on to 351 for 9 which was achieved after just two and a half hours.

So the hundred years game was finished at last. Harry Morton, the Bures captain, made a special casket, burned the bails and deposited them within, presenting them as a trophy to be contested by the two sides in perpetuity. Sadly, however, the fixture has lapsed and the East Anglian Ashes are believed to be somewhere in Great Bentley, a forgotten memento of an eccentric match.

7

Dukes and Stoolball in
Sussex-by-the-Sea

I feel slightly ambiguous about the prosperous counties of the South and South-East, but the first village cricket was played in Sussex, Kent, Surrey or Hampshire, even though no one is entirely sure precisely where or when.

Three hundred years ago Glorious Goodwood staged its first ever cricket match. Little is known about it. Who were the participants?

'Oh, the Duke's Eleven versus someone or other,' says the present Duke of Richmond, Lennox and Gordon, president of the Goodwood Cricket Club. He doesn't sound entirely sure. In fact the only certainty is that there is in existence a receipt for a cask of brandy presented to the players in 1702. Strong drink was almost as central to eighteenth-century cricket as heavy gambling.

The idea that the game is stiff-upper-lipped and sober-sided is a Victorian invention. Indeed the early cricketers of Sussex were as formidable at 'sledging' as Steve Waugh's Australians. When, a decade or so after the inaugural cask of brandy game, the second Duke of Richmond took the field against Mr Brodrick and his men of Peper Harow one of the rules stated: 'If any of the Gamesters shall speak or give their opinion, on any point of the Game they are to be turned out and voided in the match.' This directive did not apply to the captains themselves. It was emphatically 'not to extend to the Duke of Richmond and Mr Brodrick'. They, presumably, were entitled to speak and give their opinion on any point of the Game whenever it suited them.

Despite a certain haziness about the events of 1702 the present Duke was sufficiently sure of the anniversary to organise a three-match festival on his famous old ground at the end of August 2002. The first contest, on the Friday, was between the Duke of Richmond's Eleven and the Lord's Taverners. The following day the Duke's team ('My Eleven') played a match against Hambledon in eighteenth-century costume according to the rules drawn up by the second Duke in 1727. Finally, on the Sunday, the ducal eleven took on an MCC team captained by the club's former president and one-time Hampshire Captain, the ebullient Colin Ingleby-Mackenzie.

The second Duke's rules are reckoned, at least at Goodwood, to be the oldest laws of the game. They tried them out in 1977, the 250th anniversary of the Peper Harrow match. The present Duke, the tenth of Richmond and the fifth of Gordon, kept wicket that day and got the shock of his life when the very first ball – underarm, of course – passed the bat and went clean through the middle of the wicket without dislodging the bail. There were only two stumps under the rules of 1702. The Duke was keeping wicket without pads or gloves, which in the early 1700s had yet to be invented. As a result he barked his shins quite badly. The Oxford blue, Peter Graves, then a stalwart of the Sussex county side, fielded at cover and kept firing the ball hard and flat into the gloveless Duke with the result that his fingers were so sore that he couldn't write for a week afterwards. The Duke supposed he might have to play in the Hambledon game but rather thought he might prefer to umpire, wearing a full-skirted frock-coat, a wig and a three-cornered hat. Can't blame him.

Originally the Goodwood club drew its members from those who worked for the Duke. Indeed his biographer, John Marshall, said that the Duke's 'enthusiasm for the game influenced his choice of servants for the estate. Where possible, good cricket players were hired and they were, in addition to serving in such capacities as gardeners and coachmen, the Duke's own professionals. They were almost certainly the first real professional cricketers.'

'The third Duke had a groom who was a very good fast bowler,' said the present Duke. 'I don't think he ever saw a horse.'

Nowadays very few of the eighteen or so regulars are estate workers. Richard Geffen, the club secretary, told me that for a Sunday-only club with a standard somewhere 'between village and club' their numbers are about right. The age range is from fifteen to over sixty and the majority of the players come from a radius of not more than ten miles' distance. Last year only five of the twenty-five fixtures were away from home. Goodwood cricketers enjoy playing at home in the shade of the great house and the ancient storm-lopped cedar of Lebanon. The tree was planted as a seed in 1752 and planted out on the ground four years later.

Geffen himself teaches history and geography at a local prep school. Before that he was a teacher at the nearby Chichester High School for Boys. Over the years this has proved a useful nursery for the Goodwood club. A number of boys and teachers have been keen players and the present Goodwood captain and treasurer are both Chichester High men.

It's not just the dukes and the cedar who have long cricketing associations. The Miles family have been associated with the club for over sixty years. Jack was captain for seven years, his younger brother Arthur for four and his son Steve, the fixture secretary, for twenty. Jack's grandson Jamie has been playing for the club since 1995 and hit a fine 72 against Rottingdean. Arthur was the estate carpenter and Jack a forester before becoming an electrician. Steve works in financial services and Jamie is training to be a teacher.

The longest serving player is Peter Willmer, who has been playing for Goodwood since 1961. He has scored eight thousand runs for the club and has also excelled with the ball, once taking seven wickets for ten runs. He is a sheet metal worker with Metalcraft, a subsidiary of the Goodwood business conglomerate.

Most of Goodwood's games are against local villages and clubs although they also play the Grannies, London New Zealand and Sussex 'Over Fifties'. They first entered the Village Cup in 1998 and have progressed to the third round on three different occasions. On Saturdays and in mid-week the ground is available for hire for £110 for a day or afternoon game and £55 for an evening.

The revenue from these hirings has helped to finance a number of improvements in recent years. Electricity was introduced into the pavilion in 1988. The most important advantage from this was that it enabled the club to set up a bar. The bar, as most such clubs will tell you, is not only conducive to a more convivial atmosphere, it also brings in extra money.

Money from these two sources and other social events has enabled the club to commission new sight-screens from the local blacksmith as well as installing an artificial net, a new scoreboard, a three-ton roller and roll-on, roll-off covers. They have also been busy working on the playing surface, whose downland turf tended to produce unduly slow flat wickets. The substitution of clay-based loam has increased speed and bounce.

Relatively humdrum Sunday cricket coexists happily with the more exotic strain practised by the various dukes. Actually the heir to the Dukedom, the Earl of March, is more interested in motor sports. He has hardly played cricket since leaving Eton and turns out just once a year at Goodwood. 'He wouldn't have been any good at Waterloo,' says his father.

The second Duke, who was responsible for the early laws, was probably the most celebrated of the cricketing dukes, but the fourth Duke was one of those who backed Thomas Lord when he bought his 'rough piece of land' in St John's Wood and his successor became president of MCC. The famous 'bacon and egg' or 'rhubarb and custard' MCC colours were originally the Duke of Richmond's racing colours. They were then adopted by the Goodwood Cricket Club and finally by MCC around 1888. The present Duke is president of the Sussex County Cricket Club, and his grandmother used to turn out for a distinguished touring team called the White Heather Ladies.

'It's becoming unusual to have a club like ours which is both social and competitive,' says secretary Richard Geffen. The tendency is for their local rivals to be locked into leagues, which are still eschewed by Goodwood. And league cricket is becoming a different game. Clubs who play a lot of league cricket find it increasingly difficult to adjust to the sporting Goodwood conventions. They are used to a regulation forty or even fifty-five overs a side and none of the 'sporting declarations' calculated to produce the balanced games and close results which are so essential to old-fashioned village cricket.

Colin Ingleby-Mackenzie, a classic village cricketer by temperament, though still a much more skilful player than the average villager, let it be known that his ideal result would be for each side in his MCC versus the Duke match to score about two hundred and for victory to be achieved by the narrowest possible margin – a single wicket or a single run. He would not even be averse to a tie, he said, although ties and draws are a mystery to modern league cricketers where wins and losses are the only allowable results.

The three hundredth anniversary weekend was, like most Goodwood cricket, convivial yet competitive. No one was as devil-may-care as the present Duke who, in the days of his youth, raised a scratch side and then found three bottles of a fire-water called Pomerantzen which one of the Czars had presented to an earlier Duke. The three bottles were fed to the opening bowlers, who bowled incredibly fast for three overs but then collapsed and had to be removed from the field of play. The Duke himself suffered a broken cheekbone when a batsman hit the ball straight at him. He was in hospital for over a week.

There was be no Pomerantzen at Goodwood at the end of August and no broken bones either. Underarm bowling and only two stumps were the order of the day on the Saturday at least. The old cedar cast its benign shade across the field as it has done since 1756. The Duke of Richmond was there or thereabouts. There were proper sandwiches for tea and aristocrats and artisans mingled on the field of play just as they did in the eighteenth century. Time briefly stood still and spectators were tempted to believe that there'll always be an England, their England.

A few miles to the east in the tenth century King Alfred built five forts between Lewes and Chichester as part of his defences against the dastardly Danes. At the centre of these was Burpham, so named because 'burg' meant fort and 'ham' meant village. It was an important settlement in those days. Far more so than nearby Arundel. Tenth-century Burpham even had its own mint, and coins minted here have turned up at excavations in Scandinavia.

In 1980, over a thousand years after Alfred erected a great grassy rampart to protect the place, and a hundred years after cricket was first played here, the Sussex and Pakistan all-rounder Imran Khan climbed to the top of it in order to begin his run-up in a celebratory match against the village cricket team. It was possibly the most dramatic moment in the entire history of Burpham 'Burg'.

I watched a flickery video of this famous occasion in the drawing room at Frith House, snuggled under the rampart on the opposite side of the cricket ground. Frith House is the home of Lucy and Simon Brett, who moved in a year after the great centenary match played between the village and the Sussex First Eleven. Occasionally, when a batsman strikes form, balls come unexpectedly sailing over the rampart and break tiles or window-panes.

Neither Simon nor Lucy is what you would call an avid cricketer, and Simon, though he has played on the pitch and been a much-appreciated after-dinner speaker at the cricket club dinner, is positively turned off by the game's *longueurs*. However, two of his guests at that viewing were George Walker, the retiring proprietor of the local hotel and then chairman of the club, and another stalwart, the painter, former treasurer and at the time vice-president, Roger Coleman. Roger was the only person present who had actually attended the centenary match, so he was able to provide an interpretative commentary for the rest of us. Sadly much of it consisted of 'There's so-and-so – he's dead!' or 'There's so-and-so – heavens but he looks young!' Such, alas, is life.

It looked an exciting occasion with a large marquee housing a sit-down meal for over a hundred guests, a silver band which produced a fine rendition of 'Sussex-by-the-Sea', parachutists who landed on the field during tea, scores of deck-chairs and an immaculately flannelled though comprehensively outplayed home team who were first spotted early in the film as they marched two-by-two into church, presumably to be formally blessed by the vicar.

The church, whose tower is visible from the ground, now that Lucy and Simon have cleared some of their trees, is mentioned in 'Domesday Book' and has a north transept and a fine dog-tooth arch dating back to the early twelfth century. The association between church and cricket is more modern, but on the wall there is a plaque to the memory of one of the masterminds behind the 1980 celebration. This is Edward Allan Corcoran of Burpham Farm House who died only a year later. He is remembered as 'Keen Conservationist, Cricket Enthusiast and Friend to all the Village'. To demonstrate that the ecclesiastical support for cricket was continuing into the early twenty-first century there was a printed newsletter in which there was a message from the present vicar headed 'Downland Village Cup' and saying, 'I am sure you will all be interested to know that Burpham has won this knock-out competition between Boxgrove, Easebourne, Lavant, Singleton, Slindon and Walberton. The final was played at Singleton, when Burpham put up a most professional performance and defeated Easebourne by four runs – a truly exciting occasion – well done!'

Even in Burpham, I'm sorry to say, I heard rumours that the crucial run-out had been awarded after the Burpham wicketkeeper removed the bails before gathering the ball. No third umpires at the Downland Village Cup Final.

The founder of the club was E. Dawtrey Drewitt, who lived at Peppering House and laid down a ground immediately next door. Drewitt was evidently well connected. W.G. Grace was one of his playing guests and another was Sussex's dashing Indian prince K.S. Ranjitsinhji, the 'Jam Sahib'. Two other famous visitors, not particularly known for their cricket, were Cecil Rhodes and John Ruskin who, gazing out from the wicket, said that Peppering's was 'the second most beautiful view in Europe'. Rashin didn't identify his most beautiful view. He was probably just hedging his bets. 'Best' could lay him open to argument and contradiction. 'Second best' is, sort of, incontrovertible!

The club had a peripatetic history, moving from the field next to Drewitt's house to the Church Field in about 1900, then on to Peppering High Barn, where the pavilion was a shepherd's hut on wheels and where after one night of celebration the club roller vanished over the hill and ended in the water meadows, never to be recovered. The club itself spent a season or two by the river, but the field was judged too wet and they finally moved to the present ground under the rampart in 1931.

It's a sporting ground with interesting curves and slopes, and fine views quite apart from the glimpse of the church tower. It also doubles up as the home ground of the Burpham stoolball team.

This was a game about which I knew nothing until the Bretts' daily help, Jean Tester, came in at breakfast time. Jean is the widow of a former village player and groundsman, 'Tec' Tester, who died young and is commemorated on one side of the playing field, together with his friend and fellow cricket enthusiast, Spike Chitty, with a stone and two chest-nut trees.

When I met her Jean was the treasurer and chairman of the Burpham Stoolball Club and provided me with a copy of the rules and history. The game is mainly played in Sussex and East Kent with the main centre of activity, according to another well-placed source, the Duke of Richmond, around Midhurst but with curious foreign pockets of enthusiasm as far afield as Sri Lanka and beyond. Nowadays it is princi-pally a women's game. The ball is like a cricket ball but the bowling is underarm and instead of a wicket there is a raised target which the batter protects with a bat with a round blade a bit like a tennis racket. The game has been described as 'cricket up in the air', which means that unlike cricket it does not require a flat surface. Originally it was often played in churchyards and as early as the mid fifteen century parish priests are reported to have forbidden its playing in their own yard. Two hundred years later Archbishop Laud was also on record as expressing disapproval. Today the game is a model of propriety, but the reference in John Fletcher's early seventeenth-century play *Two Noble Kinsmen* (Act V, Scene ii) is certainly suggestive:

> 'Will you go with me?'
> 'What shall we do there, wench?'
> 'Why, play at stoolball.'

Hmmmm.

The great stoolball protagonist of recent times was the leading barrister Major Grantham, who single-handed brought back the Sussex smock as a suitable outfit for playing the game – a practice now, sadly, abandoned again. Some time after the First World War the Major brought a mixed team to Brighton Pavilion General Hospital where they played against a team composed entirely of inmates who had lost an arm in the conflict. On 24 September 1927 and for several years thereafter Major Grantham's Own Eleven played the Japanese Embassy at Lord's. Alas, Pearl Harbor put an end to all that and the fixture has never been resumed.

This is a digression, I suppose, but it is important to remember that the Burpham Ground is shared between the cricket and stoolball clubs. It should also be pointed out that after the last war the nearby village of Warningcamp combined forces with Burpham so that the club is now officially the Burpham and Warningcamp Cricket Club. Warningcamp may have been so called because it stands virtually in no-man's-land between the Danish invaders and the Saxon rampart, so that when the Danes could be seen wading ashore and starting to rape and pillage, a scout or two from Warningcamp could hurry up to HQ with a Warning. A more prosaic interpretation is that the Saxon chief in this settlement was a man named Warne. In any event the combined club has the head of a Saxon chief as its emblem. He is embroidered on to the stylish club flag which was stitched up by the nearby Order of Poor Clares. Unfortunately the nuns did such an intricate job that the flag is too heavy to flutter in all but the very stiffest breeze, so that it remains these days almost entirely unflown.

Through logistical incompetence I arrived at the Bretts on a day that Burpham and Warningcamp were playing an away match at historic Slindon, a club which in the early eighteenth century was regarded as the finest in all England and once humbled a combined Surrey eleven, no problem at all. Nowadays they are hardly a match for Burpham. A day earlier the Gentlemen of Warningcamp were playing the Gentlemen of Wepham, so I missed that too.

In days gone by the village played all manner of sides including the lawyers of Lincoln's Inn, the jockeys of Michelgrove and the inmates of Forde Open Prison. I was hoping the last fixture was still going because it would have been fun to see Jeffrey Archer strutting his stuff for Forde, but alas the game seems to have been dropped . . .

8

Red Roses by the Ribble plus a Yorker or Two

Even though the Heals come from Cheshire and my mother's family, the Vaughans, must have originally been Welsh, I am a child of the English South and West. I would never be so snobbish or insular as to believe that the barbarians begin somewhere just north of the Watford Gap Service Station, but I do acknowledge that I do not have to go far north of a line from somewhere around Bristol to London to feel as if I am in a foreign land. My roots are uncompromisingly southern and I am not at all sure that I don't feel foreign in Cricklewood or even Hampstead and

Highgate. I am one of what poor Francis Thompson called, in one of the greatest of cricket poems, 'the Southron folk'.

Thompson was born in Preston and died young and destitute, the victim of drugs and a melancholy homesickness graphically evoked by 'At Lord's', which Edmund Blunden himself considered the only cricketing poem that 'travels on its own power as poetry into a general anthology'. The most obvious rival is Sir Henry Newbolt's bombastic 'Vitai Lampada', which begins:

> There's a breathless hush in the Close to-night –
> Ten to make and the match to win –
> A bumping pitch and a blinding light,
> An hour to play and the last man in.

Sir Arthur Quiller-Couch, a Cornish wet-bob, included poems by both men in his first great *Oxford Book of English Verse* but neither of their cricketing efforts. Helen Gardener, who edited the next *Oxford Book of English Verse*, eliminated Newbolt altogether and restricted Thompson to just one, which was not his epic song of homesickness at Lord's. Anyway, the Newbolt is not a patch on the Thompson. In verse it's a clear victory for North over South, Preston over Clifton.

> It is little I repair to the matches of the Southron folk,
> Though my own red roses there may blow;
> It is little I repair to the matches of the Southron folk,
> Though the red roses crest the caps. I know.
> For the field is full of shades as I near the shadowy coast,
> And a ghostly batsman plays to the bowling of a ghost,

And I look through my tears on a soundless–clapping host
  As the run–stealers flicker to and fro,
  To and fro;–
O my Hornby and my Barlow long ago!

I sympathise with the sentiments but in me they are reversed. If I find myself at Headingley or Trent Bridge I feel slightly alien, far from the sights and sounds I grew up with. I feel an alien in a foreign land up north, and part of me believes that they play a different sort of cricket from grass roots to tip of the topmost tree. At base level it's been gritty competive leagues from the 1800s; at the top level it's been all Huttons and Boycotts, tough, gritty, no messing–about, no quarter given. No swashbuckling and no laughter. Oh my Compton and my Edrich long ago, long ago, Oh my Woolley and my Ames! None of that rubbish up north.

I don't know whether I believe this but it seemed only right to start in Preston, where Francis Thompson was born in 1859, at 7 Winkley Street, and where in the magnificent Harris Institute his papers are housed. There are manuscripts, including that of *Sister Songs*, as well as a number of books. A plaque to his memory is on the staircase wall, for although he left town at the age of five he is a famous son. He died in penury unlike the eponymous benefactor who made the Harris possible. This was Edmund Robert Harris, a retiring, evidently pernickety local lawyer of enormous wealth who left much of his fortune for the purpose of endowing a Free Public Library which has been described as 'one of the finest provincial Athenaeums in Europe'.

I mention this because the Harris, apart from being a sort of memorial to a fine cricket writer and lover of the game, is also the epitome of part of my idea of the north of England.

It is amazingly ostentatious – vast, imposing, a celebration of new Victorian wealth and a memorial to a fabulously wealthy person of whom virtually no one has ever heard. It has nothing to do with village cricket but everything to do with the North, or my idea of it. It is about the Industrial Revolution, Jack being as good as his neighbour and defiantly about 'brass' if not, in this case, 'muck'. Self-made triumphalism is what the Harris is about. The building is a shout of defiance to the effete tribes on the other side of the Trent. Or maybe even south of the Thames and the Severn.

I am not going to budge in my belief that the great towns and cities of the North are quite unlike their southern counterparts. I had always thought that this Great Divide extended to village level, so I assumed as I embarked on a fact-finding tour of Lancashire villages that I would encounter similarly strange and foreign communities.

In the first village I sat drinking strong tea between Albert Yates and Hughie Hunter, two of the older inhabitants, watching as icy rain skidded across the pitch and the opening bowler, a teenager from Brisbane, who was doing part-time bar work at the Eagle and Child, slipped as he delivered a ball and fell over, only to be hit hard on the arm by a fierce straight drive from the opening batsman. The ground used to belong to Lord Derby but was taken over by the Church who, for a time, placed a ban on Sunday cricket. I could see church and rectory beyond the far end of the ground and found that many of the names in the churchyard gravestones and the memorials on the walls within were those of families who had played for the village team. Even today the Hiley brothers were bowling from opposite ends once the injured Australian had gone off. Their father was in the score-box and their mother was responsible for the afternoon teas.

In the second village I found that they had the only grass wicket in the league, that its preparation was the captain's responsibility and they took a special pride in the brushing and rolling. I was shown the beautiful field by a farmer whose family formed the club in an alliance with the Berry family, who owned the famous chair-works, founded a hundred and fifty years earlier. He, John Stott, told me how his family walked their sheep through the village for twenty-one years till foot-and-mouth put a stop to it. And there was a Wednesday league team which often spent more time in one of the village's three pubs eating pies and peas and drinking Bodingtons – 'two hours cricket and four in the pub' – and the tradition was that the visiting team always batted first in case one or two of their men turned up late and they couldn't field a full eleven for the first half an hour or so.

And in the third village which had a real village green overlooked by a church and pub I met the local vicar, who until the year before had been the club secretary as well, and he took me off to a delicious tea with cake and scones and meringues made by the wife of Dick Wilson, who was such an elder statesman of the club that he was able to show me a letter from none other than Prince Philip congratulating him on fifty years in village cricket. But there was, they agreed, a drawback to such picture postcard prettiness because the village was now so popular that young people could no longer afford to live there. This meant that the cricket team came from far and wide because there weren't enough youngsters in the village to make up an eleven.

In other words though all three villages were within an hour of the Francis Thompson manuscripts in the magnificent Harris Athenaeum they could – couldn't they? – have been anywhere in England. And if they couldn't, then their cricket clubs could, for they seemed exactly, given a tiny quirk or two, like any village club I'd come across in Cornwall or Sussex or Somerset or Surrey. Some of them spoke with a slightly different accent and when they offered you a cup of tea they asked if you'd like 'a brew', but the essence, the heart of these places here in darkest Lancashire, was just as it would have been in the far-off, foreign South.

The villages were Mawdsley, Chipping and Wrea Green, and I plucked them more or less at random from the Lancashire section of the draw for the Village Cup.

Perhaps the randomness yielded a loaded result because after I'd been there I learned, from the *Shell Book of English Villages*, that Chipping is 'understandably the favourite village of many Lancashire folk because it contrives to remain a working community despite the temptation to pander to the visitors who flock to admire the cobbled courtyards, the alleyways, and the traditional cottages with stone porches and mullioned windows'.

The 'working community' is largely made possible by the prosperous Berrys' chair-works which was jointly responsible for founding the cricket club in 1950. The Berrys are Lancastrians, but their co-founders the Stotts are Yorkshiremen, so the club crest has both the white rose of Yorkshire and the red of Lancashire. Surely the only such badge in England?

Chipping *is* a very pretty village. The thirteenth-century church of St Bartholomew, by whose gate I met John Stott, has additions and refinements from the sixteenth, eighteenth and nineteenth centuries and is as immaculately maintained as the finely coiffed yew trees in the graveyard. The Sun Inn on the corner of Windy Street, where the cricketers meet for their pies, peas and pints, has high stone steps up to the entrance and a ghost called Lizzy Dean. Poor Lizzy was a serving wench engaged to a local. (I'd like to be able to say that he was a cricketer but this was more than a hundred years before the club was founded.) On the morning of her wedding in 1835 she heard the church bells ringing and looked out of the window to see her fiancé emerging from St Bartholomew's with another bride on his arm. The distraught Lizzy hanged herself in the attic. Her final request was that her body should be buried under the church path so that her false fiancé had to walk over her grave every Sunday. Whether or not she appears after the cricket dinners is unclear, but she is a widely accepted vision.

Wrea Green, where Jack Wixon is the cricketing vicar, is just as attractive and historical. It was originally called Ribby-with-Wrea, and Ribby or Rigbi was mentioned in Domesday when the local bigwig, Roger de Poictou, provided tithes of colts, calves, lambs, goats, pigs, wheat and cheese to the Priory of Lancaster as food for all the monks. Ribby or Rigbi was Norse for 'Ridge Settlement' and Wray meant 'Corner Nook'. The place was known as plain 'Wray' until the vicar, the Revd R.S. Stoney, complained that his mail was always being misdirected to the village of Wray near Hornby. Hence Wrea Green.

In recent years Wrea Green has won the prize for Lancashire's best kept village with almost monotonous regularity. The Grapes, where I met the vicar for lunch, is, in effect the cricketers' club-house as well as being an excellent pub in the normal sense of the word.

They have been playing cricket here for more than a hundred years, while the club at Fylde (town not village) just a few miles away was founded in 1810 so that, as one Fylde president, Colonel Watson, remarked, 'We were playing cricket here when Napoleon was making a nuisance of himself.'

At one time there were three duck ponds on the green, but at the request of the cricketers some time around 1900 two of them were filled in in order to create a level playing field. The surviving pond is known locally as 'The Dub', which is almost certainly a corruption of 'Daub', because that is what the villagers dug out of the ponds in order to build their old 'daub and wattle' cottages.

It's a really pretty place – perhaps too pretty in the opinion of Dick Wilson, the club's elder statesman, whose wife provided the wonderful cream tea. Dick remembers that when he was a young man 'all the locals would turn up after tea and barrack the umpires.' It doesn't happen any more because there are far fewer locals. Pretty places such as Wrea Green have become distinctly pricey and young people can certainly no longer afford to live there.

There have been similar and massive changes over at Mawdsley, where basket-making used to be the major occupation when Albert Yates and Hughie Hunter were boys. At one time the cricket club was actually known as 'The Basketmakers'. Not any more. The two men talked nostalgically of the 'twig fields' but the twig fields have all vanished and most of the working villagers commute to work in places like Ormskirk, which is the nearest substantial town.

Hughie Hunter, the club president, was a mine of information about Mawdsley and its history. His predecessor Bert Moss, who died a year short of his ninetieth birthday in

1999, used to say that there was cricket in the village back in the 1880s but no one has been able to come up with any documentary evidence for this. The club really became structured and formalised in 1898, when they joined the West Lancashire League which played in an area towards Blackburn, sixteen miles away. In 1909 they left this league when they were invited to join the Southport and District Amateur League.

There is an observable north-south divide here. Leagues were the Victorian norm up north but not down south. Hugh also pointed out that all but two of the eight teams in the first division and all seven in the second were town-based teams. One of the village teams, Hesketh Bank, dropped out in the second year of the competition and were replaced by a club called 'Ormskirk Churchmen'. I love the idea of the Ormskirk Churchmen but it does have an unmistakeable aroma of the North. Ormskirk is such an uncompromisingly gritty northern name and the idea of the Ormskirk Churchmen seems similarly un-southern. I simply can't imagine the Salisbury Churchmen or the Truro Churchmen as a cricket club. This is probably prejudice pure and simple, but I still feel that the Ormskirk Churchmen are pure Peter Tinniswood.

Bert Moss's father Tom played in the early years and can be seen in the photograph of the 1913 side that won the Sandhurst Shield which was, and is, the League's main knock-out competition. They must have been hot stuff in those early years because they had two teams in the league (the seconds played in the third division) and won the first division championship in 1912. At a reception to celebrate the event the vicar, the splendidly named Revd Lord, said that 'he found as a result of two years observation of cricket that the game was strictly played. He observed it most keenly and he was glad to bear testimony to it.' He went on to say that cricket was good for the men of Mawdsley because it gave them something to look forward to and because it enabled them to 'mix with men'. And he was obviously a great supporter of the league system. 'If they were not members of the league they would simply stick at Mawdsley and never get away.' (applause)

There were four Spiby brothers playing then, and one, Jack, was vice-captain to J.T. Southworth, whose great-great-grandson was playing for the club in 2003. Jack Spiby's brother, Geoff, was captain during the war years and carried off the league batting and bowling prizes. The Spibys are one of the great Mawdsley families. Their graves are in the churchyard and their memories survive on in the cricket field next door.

The best of all the Mawdsley men was Jack Iddon, an all-rounder who played for Lancashire and England and hit forty-six first-class hundreds. It was widely believed that Iddon would have captained Lancashire immediately after the Second World War but he was killed, tragically, in a car crash in 1946. In the thirties he'd presented a bat every year to the outstanding village player. He is commemorated in photographs in the Mawdsley pavilion.

Iddons and Spibys are part of the warp and weft of Mawdsley cricket, and there are other families who crop up regularly in the annals of the local game and on the gaunt headstones in the churchyard just a six-hit from the village wicket. There is even a poem, composed by a local 'Anon' on an unknown date.

> There will always be a cricket team
> Of 'good old Mawdsley stock'

Where village lads, also their dads
Have had their 'merry knock'.
The Southworths and the Iddons,
The Spibys, Howards too,
The Werdens, Haltons, Bridges
Only mentions just a few.

Those days are now a memory
Near forty years ago,
When the grand light-hearted banter
Greeted batsmen to and fro.
I'm sure today it's much the same
The spirit and fun;
Such pleasure got from every game,
Be it 'Lost or Won'.

As time slips by we often try
To picture this old scene,
When to cheerful yell the wickets fell
On many a village green.
Still we've had our day,
We regret to say,
To age we all must yield;
Though 'Bent and Lame' we'd like a game
On Mawdesley Cricket Field.

Not exactly in the Francis Thompson league perhaps, bearing much the same relationship to his verse as village cricket to the 'first-class' game, but well worth its place for all that.

Times *have* changed in some respects. None of the early team members could write and one of the Spiby brothers, Bert, who was secretary for many years, had to get the help of the village schoolmistress to compose the minutes. Hughie Hunter believes this same woman to have also been the scorer too.

During the Second World War the cricket ground was ploughed up – except for the square which was spared as sacrosanct. Hughie Hunter remembers the relaying and rolling of the ground in 1946, a task executed by some thirty men and boys with a borrowed roller.

There have always been ups and downs in Mawdsley cricket. Men come and men go; fine players retire. Enthusiasm waxes and wanes. The club was almost down and out in 1927. There was another collapse in 1936, when four of the better players were ensnared by the nearby Leyland Motors team, bribed with steady jobs in the motor industry. They closed during the war, revived, prospered until 1957, when another exodus provoked a collapse. The club staggered on for the next few years thanks to the strict stewardship of Bert Moss who was a pretty mean treasurer (he had to be) for thirty-two years; to Bill Leyland, a one-time red-haired fast bowler and farm labourer who became the much-loved groundsman, a renowned Lancashire 'pitch doctor' and professional groundsman at Wigan; and to John Bridge, arguably the best batsman ever to come out of Mawdsley, who continued to play until sixty-two when in retirement he used to relive every game he had ever played in until he died in his late eighties.

Hughie Hunter himself is the kind of man without whom village cricket would not survive. 'I have been dead keen on it from a young age without being much good at it,' he told me. His best claim to fame was being opening bat for the second eleven when they won the third division championship in 1961. For twenty-eight years he was the club secretary. He began a long career as a League Executive

Member in 1969 and was successively vice chairman, chairman and, from 2000, president of his own club. Since he retired in 1993 he has helped keep the outfield mown and the hedge cut. After retiring as a player in 1970 he became a league umpire and continued until a hip problem forced him to retire from that too in 1998.

Since the late nineties the playing standards have declined a little though they have strong sides at Under Eleven, Under Thirteen, Under Fifteen and Under Eighteen levels. Nowadays, he says, the eighteen-year-olds tend to go off to college or university and never come back. Others simply lose their zest for the game. Not Hughie Hunter, though. Despite never being much good, on his own admission, he has loved the game all his life and devoted much of it to his village cricket club. In this he is typical not just of Mawdsley cricketers or of Lancashire village cricketers or even Northern village cricketers, but of English village cricketers everywhere.

The co-existence of the red and white roses on the Chipping cap badge is a unique and unexpected conjunction, for few rivalries are as intense as that between Lancashire and Yorkshire. That gritty old Yorkshire writer, J.L. Carr, once quoted the great Yorkshire all-rounder, Roy Kilner, on the subject of Roses contests: 'Let there be no umpires and then Fair Cheating all round.' Carr obviously approved of this and so, I suspect, would many Lancastrians and Yorkists. To those on opposite sides of the Pennines the two are chalk and cheese. Yet to one, like myself, who is a paid-up member of the 'Southron folk' they tend to be difficult to distinguish. They seem to have many more similarities than differences and they're not like us at all. Or are they?

They are certainly passionate about their cricket. In North Yorkshire alone there are regularly more than forty entrants in the Village Cup – so many that the area has to be divided in two so that there is a North Yorkshire (North) and a North Yorkshire (South). In 2001 there were forty-three competing clubs, in 2003 there were thirty-seven. There are some wonderful sounding fixtures, none more so than that between Bolton Percy and Burton Leonard, who sound like two walk-on parts in a pastiche Shakespeare play or a couple of confidence tricksters in a twenties thriller. They are not regular rivals, Bolton Percy being a member of the York Senior League where, to the consternation of many of their rivals they were, in the eighties, the first league side to import foreign professionals. The two concerned were young Australians, one of whom stayed on and married a local girl. When I asked Ian Russell, the Bolton Percy secretary, how his side had fared, he shrugged and said that they never got very far in the Cup and that Burton Leonard were both literally and figuratively in a different league.

This is possibly true. Burton Leonard are part of the Nidderdale Amateur Cricket League and claim to have been playing since 1796, when they took part in a nine-a-side game against Knaresborough. This was for a prize of £20 and Burton Leonard won by seven wickets. Even the *Leeds Intelligencer* failed to report any cricketing activity in the village until 1852, when they came to Harrogate and played an exciting game which Harrogate won by two runs and a single wicket. It was a two-innings game and the scores were on the low side – 69, 77, 48 and 38. Afterwards they adjourned for dinner at the Ship, though it was said of the Harrogate club that 'intemperance is prohibited'. There was also a rule that no new member could be admitted without the approbation of two-thirds of the existing membership.

Today Burton Leonard puts out two senior Saturday sides, two senior evening sides, five junior sides for ages between nine and seventeen and a ladies' team.

The most successful North Yorkshire side in the 2003 Village Cup was Staxton, who made a habit of pulling off spectacularly narrow victories. They beat local rivals Flixton and Folkton by a single run in the group final, a result which apparently came amid maximum confusion and some acrimony. It was one of those nail-biting occasions when the fielding side thought the ball was dead but the batsmen scampered a winning run during the celebrations and secured the benefit of the doubt. This seems to happen in village cricket rather more than at county or Test match level. In the next round Staxton had a more emphatic win against Houghton Main of the South Yorkshire and Humberside group, defeating them by two wickets. It was one of those rather unfair sounding wins, in that Houghton Main scored 171 for 4 batting first, while Staxton admittedly outscored them but lost twice as many wickets in doing so. It didn't do them much good, though, for they lost to Streethouse, the champions of West Yorkshire, by 62 runs in round seven. Streethouse scored 206 for 9 and Staxton got 144, also for nine wickets.

There were other wondrous sounding fixtures – none more so than Ingleby Greenhow against Middleton Tyas or Knaresborough Forest against Sheriff Hutton Bridge.

I conjured up a gloriously romantic vision of Sheriff Hutton Bridge and their cricket team, picturing them as classic no-hopers, scarcely able to field a full team, playing on a rough field with nettles and cow-pats, bordering the eponymous bridge over the local stream.

Then I clocked on to reality and discovered that at the time of writing they were joint leaders of the Hunters York and District Indoor League and had been champions of the Premiership in the same estate agents' Outdoor League during the summer of 2003. Two of their stars had returned to their smart and well-appointed club-house to present trophies. These were the professional footballers, Darren Dunning and Aron Wilford, who, when not donning their whites to play cricket for Sheriff Hutton Bridge, are playing in the league for York City.

It just shows how you can be fooled by distant first impressions and exotic names, and how unpredictable and yet comforting village cricket can be. Even in Yorkshire!

9

A Revival, Tall Tales and a Big Hit

My idea of 'up north' is perversely southern so that it includes places which are geographically to the north of my world but actually have a 'southern' feel: like Hereford.

It was Matthew Engel who alerted me to Eardisland. Matthew is one of those rare cricket writers who are also proper old-fashioned journalists. He is smart enough to have been editor of *Wisden* and Washington Correspondent of the *Guardian*, an enviable though entirely deserved hack's double-whammy. When not being a foreign correspondent he lives in what sounds like bucolic bliss in Herefordshire, a county of which I am sadly ignorant though I think of it as the acme of a certain sort of Stanley Baldwin–Chesterbelloc Englishness – all black-and-white villages, eponymous cattle and draft cider. But not 'southern'.

I felt Matthew would be certain to know of a quintessential village cricket club in his adopted county, and so it transpired, though, as I should have known, it turned out to have the Engelian characteristics of being at one and the same time apparently conventional but actually unique.

Matthew had met a sociologist called Paul Selfe at the annual party given by Jeremy Bugler, an old Fleet Street hand, who had turned to TV and based himself, unexpectedly, somewhere near Hereford. Conversation had turned to cricket and Paul Selfe told him that the cricket club in his local village, after lying dormant for the best part of half a century, was being resuscitated and would, in 2002, undertake its first full season of fixtures.

'Good story,' thought Matthew. The prevailing pattern, surely, was for village cricket teams to be gradually passing away but here in the middle of Herefordshire was a community that was bucking that trend.

And so I came to Eardisland.

The village is between Leominster and the Welsh border, a part of the world I have always thought of as a world apart, *sui generis*, immune from or at least resistant to outside influence. This cannot, of course, be entirely true but I do, nevertheless, feel that if there were one spot in all England where village cricket was to be growing in popularity, this would be it. The black and white houses flank a fast-flowing stream; there is a unique eighteenth-century dovecote and, more esoterically, a rare pre-war AA box. Eardisland is achingly picturesque in a way peculiar to this very English part of England.

Paul Selfe lives off the main road between Knighton and Leominster which cuts him off from the the village and from the village's great house, Burton Court. A year or two before I met him he had retired from his teaching job in Ludlow and embarked on an oral history project. Not knowing many of the village's inhabitants, he decided that the best way to get started on this was − as it often is − to put out the word through the local pub, and so one weekend a small group of interested parties convened in the bar of the Swan Inn.

As a result a second meeting was arranged, this time with tape recorders. The whole exercise was deliberately random and informal, so much so that Selfe isn't entirely sure how his chat with one old woman came round to cricket. He supposes that he must have asked her what part sport played in village life and remembers that she began to talk about the bowls club which was a traditional centre of community life. From there she progressed to reminiscing about the old cricket meadow with its two tennis courts, its bowling green and its pavilion, where her father had turned out for Eardisland in the twenties and thirties.

Paul Selfe had no idea what she was talking about nor where it was. There had been no cricket in the village since he arrived from London about ten years earlier. However, when she explained, he knew exactly where the meadow was.

'You mean the field with the footpath through it? The one I use as a short-cut when I walk up to the village?'

Next time he walked across it he looked at the field through different eyes, and realised that it could have been a splendid cricket ground: flat as a billiard-table and perfectly proportioned. Now, however, there was no trace of cricket. It was pasture, grazed by cows.

The present owners of Burton Court are the Simpson family who bought the house in 1950. Their predecessors were the Clowes (pronounced Clews) who had been Lords of the Manor of Eardisland since 1863. Theirs was a typical story of landed gentry of the time. Young Master Peter grew up in the house, joined the Army, married, rose to the rank of Colonel, was a figure in the county. He and his wife had a son, Warren, destined one day to inherit the estate, farm it like his father and do all the county things like sitting on the bench, reading the lesson at mattins, representing the Crown and generally cutting a dash and setting a muscular Christian example to the people of Herefordshire. Alas, Warren was killed in 1918 at Amiens. The broken-hearted parents lived out their declining years in fading gentility and a slowly crumbling house. Colonel Peter died first and his widow followed in 1950, when the estate was sold off in parcels with the house and garden passing to the Simpsons.

Paul Selfe's researches revealed that the cricket began in 1866, three years after the Clowes first came to Eardisland. It was a fairly feudal affair, more country house cricket than the village variety, with the teams composed almost entirely of the family, their guests and friends, and workers from the estate. Then gradually more and more local people joined in and the club became more and more Eardisland and less Burton Court. Even so the ground belonged to the Cloweses and a familiar ritual was the arrival of the team teas by horse and cart, complete with urn from the big house.

The old club folded in the 1960s, for reasons that are not entirely clear. The oldest survivor from it was Harry Davis, who had opened the batting and was a gardener in the thirties.

The researches by Paul Selfe and his team led to the publication of an engaging and exhaustive work of local history and also to a renewed interest in the old cricket club. Since 1996 appeared to be the 130th anniversary of the original foundation of the club the modern Eardislanders decided to play a great anniversary match. There were more than enough volunteers to make up two teams, so the animals were cleared off, a strip was cut, and a marquee hired, along with a fire-eater and a bouncy castle. It was so much fun that a similar match was played the following year and the year after, when they had so many cricketers that they played sixteen-a-side.

In the Swan some time in 1999 it was agreed that if the village could muster thirty-two players then it really would be worth getting up a regular team. Feelers were put out, soundings were taken, Darren Jones, the Swan's landlord was elected captain, but then the owner of the old cricket meadow said he wasn't prepared to turn his pasture over to regular cricket. Luckily another farmer who had already played in the anniversary games offered a nearby field of his own. In September 2001 this was cleared, flattened and sown with grass-seed. When Paul Selfe showed it to me two weeks later on a showery Saturday morning the ground was more green than brown, promising good turf for Eardisland's first full season for about forty years.

The new Eardisland ground was opened on Sunday, 2 June 2002, patriotically coinciding with the euphoria of the Queen's Golden Jubilee celebrations. In the morning there was a Kwik-Cricket competition involving sixty local school-children, all of whom received a certificate from Bill Wiggin, MP for the Leominster constituency in which Eardisland lies. Mr Wiggin, for his part, got a bottle of claret from Ian Watson, the club secretary, and was mistaken, by Martyn Connop, the chairman, for the conjuror and children's enter-tainer. As the conjuror arrived in a smart vintage limousine flying the cross of St George this was perhaps understandable. The chairman suspected something was wrong when he noticed the newcomer was wearing a gaudy waistcoat, a yellow shirt and green trousers with Union Jack stickers on his spectacles, but only fully realized his mistake when his guest removed an egg from his ear and said he had come to amuse the children.

The celebratory match was between the Oral History team, drawn from Paul Selfe's local history group, and an invitation squad under the non-playing captaincy of Howard Davies. These were the teams that had first met in 1996 to mark 130 years of cricket in Eardisland. The first three years' games were played in superb weather but there followed three years of rain, thunder and lightning. Happily the weather on this glorious second of June was fine, though the wind was high and the erection of the gazebos (aka tea tents) was fraught and hazardous.

Howard Davies won the toss and put the Historians in to bat. The number participating in the game was always difficult to predict, but on this occasion worked out at fifteen a side. Local Eardisland rules dictated that all who wished to participate should be allowed to do so. The game was to be twenty-four overs a side and the Eardisland Bat, which for most of the year hangs in the Swan pub, was to be presented to the Man of the Match.

The Historians opened soundly and accelerated when Chris Watson and Hugh Lowe (a once-a-year player who drove with great power before being bowled for 10 by a seamer from Andrew Davies) came in at seven and eight. In true English tradition the middle order collapsed with four batsmen going in four overs for five runs. There was then a brief flurry from a Great Britain international Aussie Rules footballer and a classy debut from a Zimbabwean called Alastaire Munns, newly arrived in the village. The last three batsmen added much needed respectability to the score with Edward Simpson, just back from trekking in the Himalayas, eschewing the Wellington boots and shooting jacket in which he had played in the previous year's stormy fixture. Paul Selfe, convenor of the Oral History group, came in last and, fittingly, top scored with 12. When he was last out just before tea the Historians had made 77 off their full twenty-four overs.

Alastaire Munns, the newly arrived Zimbabwean, got a wicket with his first ball and also provided some much-needed athleticism in the field. Paul Selfe who wrote the match up for the Eardisland newsletter then described a catch at deep mid-wicket by his team-mate Edward Simpson, the Himalayan trekker, which is in the best tradition of *England, their England.*

Edward had been quenching his thirst and examining the quality of the grass in the outfield, when the ball approached in a high trajectory against a strong sun. Aware that all eyes were on him and the batsmen had already crossed for two speedily taken runs, Edward moved back towards the boundary edge and then shuffled to his left. As he stumbled the ball reached his left shoulder, causing him to readjust, but he was unable to retain his equilibrium. There was a possibility that the ball could have struck him a severe blow on the head, but dancing lightly to his left as if in a tango-mode he plunged forward and took the catch. Although not cleanly. The ball flew into the air and over his right shoulder. But turning his imaginary partner 90 degrees he fell back and held the ball as it plummeted towards

the earth. He stood, covered in grass with the ball raised
in his hand. A sensational catch.

It is such moments, particularly when described like that,
which, for me, define village cricket. In the end, however,
the catch proved of no avail for the Davies team eventually
ran out winners by one wicket with two balls to spare.

If you can't manage a tie then that is just about the next
best thing. Andrew Davies won the Eardisland Bat. Not long
afterwards Sam Gittoes, who opened for the Historians and
was run out for 2 before taking two wickets with his accomplished leg-breaks, was selected for Herefordshire Under Tens
against Shropshire.

In the newsletter Paul Selfe wrote that 'Tim Heald was
impressed to find that such a small village could re-establish
a thriving club which began in 1866, nearly forty years after
the last one folded.'

I *am* impressed. Very.

Hagley, near Stourbridge in the West Midlands, claims to be
the oldest club in the Midlands. Like so many others it began
as the private fiefdom of an aristocratic family and yet is now
undeniably a bona fide community club based on the local
village. The Lyttelton family, who were accustomed, scan-
dalously, to taking over the long gallery of their ancestral
home as a sort of indoor net, were also using the field as a
private ground for themselves and their friends long before
the club was first formed in 1834. The club history describes
them as 'a family whose name is interwoven in English Cricket
history, and who have supplied more entries in *Wisden* than
any other'.

George Lord Lyttelton, who built the present Hagley Hall,

was private secretary to Frederick Prince of Wales, who was not only killed after a blow to the head from a cricket ball but was also the first president of the Surrey County Cricket Club.

On one famous occasion in 1867 they fielded an entire Lyttelton XI against the nearby Bromsgrove School and beat them by a handy ten wickets on the Hagley ground. I am indebted to the club history for the full score-card and report, which diverges from the testimony of the present Lord Cobham (head of the Lyttleton clan), who told me on an earlier occasion that the match in which eleven Lytteltons played was against Malvern College and was lost. Lord Cobham is always an entertaining witness, but sometimes an erratic one.

The 1867 parish magazine said that 'This peculiar event, which it is sad to reflect, the History of the World can in all probability contain but once, has passed off with great success in the presence of a very large gathering from the neighbourhood.'

Bromsgrove won the toss and 'took the willow', making a respectable 150, 'His Reverence' (the Hon. Revd W.H. Lyttelton) catching the eye as a nimble cover-point. 'The family then girt themselves for the fray, the peer and C.G. being the first to appear. After some fine hitting by the latter the former had to retire without cracking his egg.' There was then some mighty hitting, especially from S.G., who made 51, and A.V., who got 46 including 'a glorious off-drive for five'. Bromsgrove then batted a second time and 'tried again what they could do against the slows of C.G. and the fast of N.G. and didn't make much of either'. They were all out for 51. 'Each of the little 'uns ran out a man,' reported the parish magazine, 'N.G. and

E. went in to get the dozen requisite, the latter being a candidate for the barnacles. This disaster he however averted scoring a capital seven not out, the other three. Thus the family won by ten wickets amidst the cheers of the numerous spectators, and the congratulations of their backers and friends.'

In celebration a poem was composed, the first verse of which, supposedly by Lord Lyttelton himself, ran

> Sing the song of Hagley Cricket
> Come what ere eleven may
> Quoth the Peer 'My boys shall lick it
> My eight boys shall win the day.'

The association between club and family has always been close. Hagley still plays on the family ground and Viscount Cobham is still the president. Even in 1867, however, the team was by no means all-Lytteltonian. In the first match of the 1867 season, for instance, when they beat long-standing local rivals Belbroughton by an innings, there wasn't a single Lyttelton in the Hagley team.

Nor was every member of the family besotted with the game. When Spencer, the youngest of the eight Victorian Lyttelton brothers, asked his stepmother where his cricket ball was, she, Sybella, replied with some asperity, 'In the baby's perambulator where it belongs.'

In 1977 Viscount Cobham, sometime President of MCC and Governor-General of New Zealand, quoted the novelist Thomas Hardy as saying that 'A village is nothing unless it is built around a church.' Cobham seemed mildly scandalized by this as Hardy was widely believed to be an atheist, but the Viscount put his own spin on the matter by declaring 'In the sense that a Church is an institution which brings people together it is obviously a good thing, but the same is possibly no less true of a cricket ground and happy indeed is the village which can boast both a church and a cricket ground on, so to speak, the same campus.'

Quite so. Given the choice between church and cricket I feel pretty sure which this particular Viscount would have preferred. He once declared:

> It is sometimes forgotten in these fiercely competitive days of averages and publicity that cricket is basically played for fun and this I feel has never been forgotten where Hagley is concerned. In that sense village cricket is the purest of all the forms of cricket. It is played in the spirit for which cricket was invented. When J.M. Barrie said that it was an idea of the gods he can not have visualized some of the modern Test matches being played against a hideous cacophony of howls, banging tins, jeers and yells, and short-pitched bowling being flung at the opposition's head at a rate of thirteen overs an hour. These things have never disfigured Hagley cricket and I am quite certain that they never will.

I am sure that Lord Cobham's certainty was well-founded, but it was about the time that he expressed his strong opinions that the leagues came to this part of the world and the Hagley club duly signed up. For more than twenty years the village team played in the Worcestershire Border League. At the very end of the twentieth century they actually won this and as a consequence the present Lord Cobham, son of the Governor-General, wrote to say, 'I have to report that Hagley have become terribly smart having gained promotion to the

Birmingham League. I view this prospect with some concern as sight-screens and wicket covers are "de rigueur" and hardly in keeping with a Grade 1 Park.' A few months later he wrote again to say that the Hagley Cricket Club's 'foray into the league has proved somewhat short-lived, having suffered the ignominy of demotion'.

I have to say that he sounded rather relieved.

In fact they earned a reprieve but came bottom of the Birmingham League again. Their retiring captain and high-scoring batsman, Andy Hadley, said they had fallen foul of the professionalism of the Birmingham League, not having the money to pay a 'major' overseas player like some of the others. Others obviously felt the same, for their old friends and rivals from 1867, Belbroughton, formed a small league of like-minded communities to play matches in a friendlier fashion. I can't help feeling that this is what the Lytteltons of yesteryear would have wished. One doesn't like to think of them all spinning in their graves.

A certain sort of village cricketer's only serious ambition is to hit huge sixes. Albert Trott, Arthur Wellard, Ian Botham and Freddie Flintoff have a lot to answer for. My father was like that, and so was Michael Meyer, the Ibsen Scholar, who did it at Stockholm and the Hague. So too was Bob Scott, later Sir Robert, the man who headed Manchester's Olympic bid, got them the Commonwealth Games and then defected to Liverpool, where he masterminded their attempt to become European City of Culture.

Although I never saw him play cricket at university, where I first knew him, I sensed that he would have performed in the bucolic, swashbuckling style of the six-hitters above. He was a burly fellow in those days and an accomplished actor.

I remember Maria Aitken, who was playing opposite him in some OUDS production, saying that when they had to embrace in rehearsals she could just about get her arms round him in the morning; but not after lunch. Bob was involved in the famous Elizabeth Taylor Oxford production of *Dr Faustus* and got to know Taylor and her then husband Richard Burton. Years later I was interviewing Burton on the set of *Where Eagles Dare*. It was morning but we were already on the vodka in Burton's dressing-room and getting on well – too well for the liking of Burton's PA, who was making it quite clear that Burton must get rid of this increasingly over-familiar hack because there was a very important person waiting to see him and he shouldn't be kept waiting. Eventually an exasperated Burton told the PA to show in the important visitor whereupon the door opened and in walked Bob.

After we had stopped laughing we all had another vodka and then went off for a jolly lunch at a restaurant called, I think, the Thatched Barn. I still don't know how Bob had persuaded Burton's acolytes that he was 'important'. As far as I was concerned he was just 'Bob'. I am amazed and impressed that although I continue to think of him simply as 'good old Bob', he has convinced so many others, including the great and the good, that he is as the Burton people believed, a genuine VIP!

When I first knew him Bob seemed the quintessential southerner and I was surprised when he went up north and became so closely identified with that part of the world. He also lost a lot of weight, and I was afraid that with the publicity and his knighthood he might have got grand. However, he still seemed a good person to ask about the mysteries of village cricket north of the Watford Gap, and it was a huge relief when he answered my query with the words: 'I used to play village cricket for a place called Charlesworth in Derbyshire [while working in Manchester] and we played wonderfully named villages like Broadbottom and Tintwistle. Indeed it is one of my proudest boasts that I am credited with the biggest six ever seen at Old Glossop – out next ball, trying again!'

Actually Charlesworth plays its cricket in a club formed by itself and the neighbouring village of Chisworth, though the Charlesworth club was founded in 1861, six years before the Chisworth men followed suit. The reason why Chisworth lagged behind was that the community was dominated by a temperance society which advocated total abstinence and deeply disapproved of the the alcohol associated with cricket. The Charlesworth club-house in those days was the Horseshoe Inn, later the Charlesworth Garage, and their annual dinners in the pub were famously 'spent in singing and dancing, with solos on the celestial organ'.

According to Doctor Shimwell, the club historian, Charlesworth's social life in those days was rather better than its cricket. They used to beat Kinder, Whitfield, Glossop and Wesleyan Amateurs, but struggled against more established sides from Hollingworth, Brookfield and Tintwistle. Chisworth, centred on a prosperous colliery, weren't much better and had difficulty beating sides such as Compstall, Mellor and Thornsett, even when they scored less than forty.

Crucial changes took place in the 1890s. Charlesworth officials attended a meeting of the North Derbyshire and Stockport District League in 1890, but after polling their members decided to stay outside the league and continue playing friendlies. Three years later the Glossop and District League was founded and again Charlesworth decided to persevere with friendlies. A year later they reversed the decision, reinforced by some members of the Chisworth club, and in 1895 the two teams were formally amalgamated.

Hitherto the club had rented a meadow next to the Gamesley railway sidings where Thomas Davenport, the landlord of the Grey Mare Inn, acted as groundsman and was reputed to roll the wicket with beer barrels before the club bought a proper roller. By 1907 members were seriously unhappy with the state of the ground and when, one day that year, the farmer turned his beasts on to the field of play after the wicket had been prepared, they decided to look elsewhere. They soon found the present ground at Bankfield and got the Derbyshire all-rounder Harry Bagshaw to lay a wicket.

In 1921 the local Howard Estate, of which the cricket field was part, came up for sale. Howard's bailiff put a price of £120 on the field and in less than a week the club had raised £123, including a £50 cheque from the president, Robert Moss. Lord Howard was so impressed that he let them have it for just a £100.

There have been changes over the years: there is women's cricket now; the old Glossop and District League has vanished, and Charlesworth now play in the Derbyshire and Cheshire League; an anonymous donor has given them a spanking new green and gold club sign; there is a successful fund-raising club which conducts a monthly prize draw at the George and Dragon; the widow Albert Ferrand left a small legacy 'to remember her first husband's name and the happy times he spent on the cricket ground'.

As always whatever material changes take place the spirit lingers on. Old men don't forget. Bob Scott still remembers his mammoth six at Old Glossop. 'That was twenty years ago,' he says, 'and another life away.'

But whatever he says, he remembers it as if it were yesterday. That's what village cricket does for you.

10

A Second Innings for the Major

I had originally thought that the epic match between the Balliol College Erratics and Major Rodney's 'motley crew', as the *Cricketer* unkindly described us in the caption to our team photograph, would be the final outing for the Major and his men. I was forty-eight after all, and that seemed a perfectly respectable age at which to hang up one's bat and boots for the last time. Besides the day turned out to be so enjoyable that to try to repeat it felt like tempting fate.

TV, however, dictated otherwise. I was happy to comply

with television's dictates and to have a compelling reason for resuscitating Major Rodney's Eleven – which was that David Taylor thought that doing so would help the series.

The original idea was that the Major and I should play Anthony Fortescue's Eleven at Boconnoc. The old deer park seemed precisely the setting the Major would enjoy, and Fortescue precisely the sort of semi-playing Duke of Norfolk figure the occasion demanded. I issued my challenge one day but then, as I have tried to explain, something went wrong and my challenge was unaccepted.

The obvious fallback was Fowey. Ground beautiful, chairman amenable, me vice-president. I approached Ed Leverton, the chairman who re-founded the club in 1973 along with Phil Johns, a fearsome fast bowler for Cornwall in the seventies and manager of the Midland Bank. Ed explained that the Fowey first team were playing away at Veryan on the Roseland peninsula one summer Sunday but that he could put together a team drawn from colleagues at work – Ed works for the English Cricket Board – from the Fowey Second Eleven and from their junior squad. I replied, truthfully, that if my sense of what Major Rodney's would be like a decade further on was accurate, then his team would be more than a match for us.

We settled on Sunday, 17 August because it was one of the few weekend days that none of the Fowey teams were playing at home. It was the opening day of the Fowey regatta which my wife thought would cause all sorts of problems to do with accommodation. This turned out not to be the case, but I did realise that August was a bad month because chaps tended to be on holiday. This, together with old age and various alleged infirmities, took care of six of my original team.

That left me with just four of the original team excluding myself. The trombone-playing, canal-boating doctor was retired and living in Bath and though dangerously advanced in years was eager to play. The twenty-year-old Sri Lankan student was now teaching biology and coaching the Under Fourteens at St Benedict's, Ealing, and though not, according to his own estimation, bowling at quite as zippy a pace as a decade earlier was nevertheless in reasonable nick. My son Tristram had become features editor of a sports/business magazine and his friend Joe was a successful commodity broker. The last two sounded alarmingly rusty, but they were anxious to perform so I inked them all on to the team-sheet.

Television stepped in to fill two of the gaps. David Taylor was adamant that, of course, this was my team and I was more than free to choose precisely who I wanted. On the other hand he was keen that Steve Hewlet should keep wicket and Joshi should be my all-round 'ringer', giving me a net beforehand and orchestrating the game whenever necessary. This he would be able to do on account of his manifestly superior skills and experience. Joshi was the Antiguan professional at Chagford, of whom we have already heard. Steve Hewlett was, as far as I was concerned, an unknown quantity in both a wicketkeeping and general non-cricketing sense.

'Who Hewlett?' I asked daringly.

I already had a wicketkeeper up my sleeve in the person of my wife's former games mistress at Adelaide's Methodist Ladies' College. Marg Jude was short but formidable, a former Olympian hockey full back who had kept wicket for the Australian women's team and opened the innings for some five different English counties, averaging over a hundred. I had sounded her out when she came to visit us in Carrickalinga earlier in the year and she was most enthusiastic especially if she was allowed to be in charge of field placing. If Marg was up for it I didn't fancy having this Hewlett fellow keeping wicket ahead of her. Class will out. Especially Australian class.

'Steve Hewlett is Head of Programmes at Carlton TV,' said David.

'Is he any good?'

'He's been scoring forties and fifties for Harpenden,' said David.

I was about to protest that this didn't really answer my question when self-interest became the better part of valour and I said that he sounded absolutely terrific, red-hot and it would be an honour to have such a man playing under my captaincy. Sir.

To be honest I wasn't entirely sure about Joshi either. David said he'd topped the West Indian batting and bowling averages in South Africa on one tour but I'd seen his bowling being torn apart by some batsmen from a small village between Plymouth and Tavistock and I wasn't so sure. But even if he was utterly brilliant was it quite cricket to have a paid professional turning out for Major Rodney's? Surely we were an amateur side?

But I swallowed hard and said nothing.

My team was now seven strong. Eleven years earlier my elder son Alexander had captained the opposition. Now he was thirty-one, author of two unpublished novels and an unpublished sit-com, and although he hadn't played a lot of cricket recently I felt I should have him on my side. Dynasties are partly what this sort of cricket is about. There is a buzz about playing cricket with different generations of the same family and it is one of the comparatively few games in which fathers, sons and even grandfathers can reasonably be expected to participate together. It seemed entirely appropriate that Major Rodney's Eleven should contain a father and two sons even if none of them was much cop at cricket. A serious purist of the 'If it's worth doing badly' school would argue that it was *particularly* appropriate if they weren't much cop at cricket.

On the other hand I must have a few real cricketers even if only to look good on TV. This is when I thought of Charles Vyvyan. Charles was a Cornishman, a cousin of Sir Ferrers, the baronet who lived in lovely Trelowarren. He was also a Balliol man who had played for the Erratics, but he was far better than that suggested, having opened for Winchester College and the Oxford University Authentics. Could have had a blue if he hadn't looked so deceptively languid. Even in the crepuscular penultimacy of his fifties he still seemed deceptively languid. He was a retired Major-General and could be relied upon to wear the sort of blazer we had lost with Hugh Massingberd. I simply had to have Charles, and Charles, bless him, agreed.

This made nine. James Coggan, the manager of Fowey's Marina Hotel, a smart bijou establishment with an award-winning chef, had volunteered to put on a post-match barbecue just as he had done after my panel performance with the Bishop of Truro and Ronnie Harwood at the du Maurier Festival. He had played at school, which was Millfield, and that in itself sounded like a qualification. I sounded him out and he appeared genuinely enthusiastic. Ten. And talking of barbecues the Bishop had come to the last one and he was always telling me how if it hadn't been for Derek Underwood he would have bowled for Kent and England in the style of the great D.V.P. 'Doug' Wright. I e-mailed the Bishop more in hope than expectation and was surprised but delighted when he rang back, thoughtfully before the start of play in the Old Trafford Test match, and said he'd be there after mattins. Eleven. We had a full team.

We were, however, disturbingly long in the tooth. Even my children and their friends were pushing or even over thirty. I toyed with the idea of Brian and Jane Perman's son Joe, who was alleged to be a nifty fielder, but at twelve perhaps he was a shade too young to be playing alongside a bishop and a sixty-something jazz trombonist. The sensible thing seemed to be to ask the sons for more mates. Alexander duly obliged by promising two Balliol contemporaries and sometime Erratics: Neil Quinlan, who now did something only semi-comprehensible for a Japanese bank, and Niru Ratnam, who after a spell as art critic of the *Face* now had his own gallery in Hoxton. Neil was apparently a cricketing duffer, but Niru was an accomplished all-rounder who, according to Alexander, would have won an Oxford blue had he not refused to give up smoking. Apparently smokers couldn't win blues in the Oxford of the 1990s. Big change from my day.

So we were thirteen. Not much margin for error and falling by the wayside, but we had a team with a reasonable balance between youth and experience, batting and bowling, skill and ineptitude. A few days beforehand Ed Leverton e-mailed. He seemed to have a similar mix except for the fact that his men were a decade or so younger. His oldest sounded as if they were still in their forties or just possibly early fifties, and his youngest were teenagers. Never mind, I consoled myself, experience will prevail, age before beauty. It did sound, however, as if his players were in practice. Most of mine were dangerously out of it.

And so the great day arrived.

I was nervous on many counts, the first of which was actually getting eleven more or less hale and hearty individuals to turn up and take the field. I remembered my opposing captain, Ed Leverton, saying how difficult it was for Fowey to field a full team in the early days of his reign. I also thought of Jack Daniel, captain of the Somerset county team, who in the twenties stood at the station barrier in Bath as the London train came in and called out, pleadingly, 'Anyone here play cricket? Somerset are a man short!'

Naturally we had several potential 'no-shows'. This is a *sine qua non* for captains who try to put together such scratch teams. I was particularly worried about those who said they were going to spend time on the beach or in the surf at Newquay. I was concerned that they might acquire serious hangovers or even set fire to Viscount Long and his wife who had been complaining in the national press about the pyromanic tendencies of late-night revellers on the beach below their holiday hide-away. It would have been embarrassing to have had members of Major Rodney's in the Newquay nick. Luckily I had a bonus and potential fall-back in that Kate Mortimer, cricketing half-blue from Oxford (Oxford didn't award blues to women any more than to smokers) agreed to be Major Rodney's scorer.

In the event the revellers turned up and the two no-shows were our potential star Niru Ratnam and James Coggan from the Marina. Shortly before the great day Niru fell off his bicycle on a tour of Hardy country and had to be stitched up in Dorchester General Hospital. Then James suddenly remembered that Sunday the seventeenth was the first day of the Fowey Regatta and the hotel was likely to be busy.

So we were back to eleven.

I turned up early at the ground, pretty and within sight of the Fowey Hall Hotel, originally built by a local lad called Charles Hanson who became Lord Mayor of London and the supposed model for Toad Hall in *The Wind in the Willows*. I was early for televisual purposes, because I first had to do a sequence with a Subbuteo type board game explaining the field-placings and then had to be filmed having a net with our ringer, Mr Joshi of Chagford. I more or less bluffed my way through the former and quite enjoyed the latter. Joshi was a good teacher and at least since school if not before I have always enjoyed lessons from those who know what they are talking about and have a gift for passing it on. Joshi did. The only problem was that it's not easy to teach such an old dog new tricks. When a man has been playing, or even more significantly *not* playing, cricket for over fifty years it is not tremendously helpful to tell him that he's holding the bat wrong or that his stance is too one-eyed. You can't undo the teaching and habits of fifty years in half an hour. You have to work with what you're given. Or as I once, in slightly different circumstances, heard Denis Compton say to Clive Radley at Lord's apropos his precocious son, 'Now don't you go coaching it out of him.'

It was obvious that Joshi was a good coach but equally obvious, I think, that I was beyond coaching. It was useful to have some balls thrown at me and to remind myself of how to hit them, but it wasn't realistic to expect to turn me into something I had never been.

By two p.m. I had a team of ten and a scorer, the redoubtable Kate Mortimer, who would have been a more than useful addition to my playing team. I had brought along a copper disc newly arrived from Rockford Wines in the Barossa valley. It had my name on one side and was blank on the other. It seemed an appropriate thing to toss with, but I was overruled by David Taylor, who said that the home captain should toss with his own coin. I hadn't properly considered the etiquette of coin tossing and deferred. Ed Leverton produced a fifty pence coin and we walked out to the wicket where Ed tossed and I called heads. This was my first defeat of the day. Ed said he'd bat, which was what I would have done myself.

We were still a man short. In fact we were a bishop short, which was even worse. Ed lent us one of his players, a keen and nimble thirteen-year-old, and I opened with Joe Cox from the estuary end. Joe bowled much as I remembered – fast and wild. At the other end Hemish Gunasekera, despite protests about his dodgy knee, bowled in the same neat whippy way that I remembered from our last match. The batsmen, however, looked mature and accomplished and in no serious trouble.

After a few minutes the Bishop hove in sight, changed into his flannels and took up position at first slip. Presently I brought him on in place of Joe Cox. His first over was tidy and cost just two runs. In the next over Hemish bowled their opening bat and an over later the Bishop had his partner lbw. Not long after that my elder son Alexander took a catch off the bowling of his old friend Hemish and at 78 for 3 off almost half their overs the home side weren't exactly strug-gling but were not running away with the match in the manner I had begun to fear. I would have been happy with anything under 175 off their forty overs.

At about half-way, however, we started to lose our way. Mel Henry GP never really found his rhythm and his four overs cost thirty-three runs. Alexander, the elder son, a reluctant bowler in any case, had one over which cost nine runs not including two wides and a no-ball. I knew that without the hors-de-bicycle Niru and the overworked hotelier I was going to have fewer bowling options than I would have wished, but at least I still had Joshi up my sleeve. This was just the situation for a ringer, but to my horror his bowling seemed as unthreatening as it had when I saw him being put to the sword by a village side near Dartmoor. He didn't look like getting a wicket and his third over cost ten.

I took him off and brought back Hemish, who though tiring continued to look the part. Joe had another three overs and then I bought the Bishop back in what seemed an inspired move. Off his very first ball he had Ed Leverton, the home captain, smartly stumped by Steve Hewlett. 'Almost like real cricket,' said Steve, wryly. In the end the Bishop bowled out the innings and ended with the remarkable figures of ten overs, three maidens and three wickets for sixteen. Hemish took a deserved 4 for 55 off fifteen.

The Fowey team batted well but we could have done with a couple of extra bowlers. Our fielding with one or two exceptions, notably Steve Hewlett behind the stumps, was pretty much a nightmare. Joshi said something disparaging to David Taylor about our inability to take catches, but this was a tad unfair as both Alexander and the General pouched the ball. It was our ground fielding which sorted the men from the boys. I took a dive fielding at deep square leg and at least won myself green grass stains on both knees of my whites, which suggested courage if not competence. I then took a bouncing ball full in the chest and tore or tweaked several muscles in my right leg. Dr Henry nearby was markedly unsympathetic, pointing out that he was now a retired doctor and could suggest nothing more helpful than ice. The older members were very slow and our throwing arms had lost whatever zing they might once have had. When I say that the fielding sorted the men from the boys I mean that in this instance the boys were better than the men.

Oh well: 209 for 7. I was not dismayed. Our batting line-up struck me as stronger than our bowling. We staged a team photograph for wives and TV (the General producing a splendid striped regimental blazer worthy of Hugh Massingberd) and enjoyed a sumptuous tea provided by Mrs Leverton and friends. Major Rodney's Eleven were relieved to have got through a hot forty overs and seemed to me to be exuding a quiet confidence. You couldn't say we were brimming with the stuff but we were not dismayed or even downhearted.

I confess I didn't give a lot of thought to the team photograph until I saw it printed out a few days later. It was revealing. In fact it spoke volumes. The first obvious point was that the old codgers, five of us, were sitting on the chairs in the front while the younger members stood behind us, thus demonstrating their relative athleticism. The second, even more obvious point, is that we are clearly not a team. We are all looking in opposite directions and keeping a more than decent distance between each other. You wouldn't think we had previously met. The General is easily the best dressed – the blazer giving him an undoubted edge – while some of the back row look distinctly scruffy.

A hundred years earlier several of us would have sported moustaches. The Bishop would have worn a dog collar instead of his open-necked shirt and possibly some eccentric canonicals in the style of Prebendary Wickham of Martock. Several of us would have worn caps, if not straw boaters. And at least a couple of us would have been sprawling languidly on the grass.

It gave me pause for thought. In this instance I have provided a fairly detailed match report, but in most of the village cricket pavilions I visited those fading team photographs on the peeling walls are almost all that survive of teams past, ghostly figures staring down at their successors. They speak generally of a gentler age, more fastidiously dressed, more elegantly posed. They all tell stories, as does Major Rodney's. I'm not altogether sure that our picture tells an entirely satisfactory tale. Indeed we look, once again, a motley crew. But if you judged us solely by the picture you would know less than everything. They say that pictures cannot lie and that a single photograph is worth a thousand words or more. In terms of cricket team photos I don't believe this is so.

We opened with the Bishop and the General. I felt I couldn't do otherwise and they looked magnificent as they walked to the wicket. The General was tall and willowy and wearing what looked like his grandfather's cream flannel trousers though he told me they came from Ralph Lauren. They weren't held up by a striped regimental tie but they gave the impression they should have been. They seemed to me to strike a shrewd sartorial-psychological blow for our team. The Bishop, a good foot shorter and considerably portlier but visibly glowing from his sterling spin bowling, was the Wise to the General's Morecambe. Appearances apart one felt that, especially after his bowling, we might have Divine Right on our side. They were a TV director's dream ticket too and as they walked out, the personification of Church and State at play, they said suitable words along the lines of 'I'll take first strike, your Grace' and 'God be with you, General.' It was all very satisfactory, especially as the next man in was the burly hero of Harpenden, wicketkeeping Steve Hewlett himself.

The General took guard, surveyed the field, and assumed the stance of a latter-day Douglas Jardine. I felt almost sorry for Ed Leverton and his team.

Play.

The bowler, Stephenson, came in, delivered the ball and General Vyvyan played an exquisite forward defensive shot, head steady as a rock, bat perfectly positioned, eyes fixed like lasers on the ball. As near perfection as a Winchester and Balliol veteran could muster.

Oh dear. How could anyone play such an elegant shot and miss the ball so completely? And was it really entirely fair that the very first ball of the innings should be so absolutely straight and on a length, so that one's wicket should be utterly, comprehensively toppled? The General turned his head, surveyed the shattered woodwork, rose from the ground-sniffing perfection of his foreword defensive shot, put his bat under his arm, turned and trudged disconsolately back towards the pavilion.

The rest of us were in shock.

'Bad luck, Charles!'

'Tough lines, General!'

'Could have happened to anyone, old boy.'

The General, naturally, took it like a man, full on the chin, made no excuses but was not best pleased.

The next man in was Steve Hewlett, who looked to me

like a biffer of the ball. Those closest to Steve intimated that he was inclined to hit the ball in the air. He looked burly enough to hit it hard, and if he was scoring forties and fifties at Harpenden then . . . well, maybe all was not lost. The first ball went for a biffed single, in the air but safe. That brought the Bishop to the striker's end. My intimations were that His Grace's batting was not as good as his bowling and I can't pretend that he looked particularly safe. However, the last ball of the over went for a streaky four and at 5 for 1 we looked wobbly but not necessarily doomed.

The next over was a nightmare. The bowler was Steve Arthur, who had already retired after hitting an undefeated fifty – I've said comparatively little about the opposition side for reasons which should be obvious. This in no way implies criticism – rather the reverse – and their Steve looked a pretty good player. Anyway he had Steve Hewlett caught and bowled off the third ball of his first over. Steve was cross with himself and rightly so. He had had too early a biff and tried to bludgeon his way out of trouble before playing himself in. It meant we were five runs for two wickets and were down to what I had already described – to camera – as our collapsible middle.

'Bad luck, Steve.'

'Tough lines, old boy.'

'Could have happened to anyone.'

The younger son Tristram strode purposefully to the wicket and nicked a single off the first ball he received.

That brought the Bishop back to the striker's end, and I'm sorry to say that he was comprehensively bowled next ball. Six runs, three wickets and looming embarassment.

I would like to be able to describe my effort in detail but it's a bit of a blur. I would have been nervous enough without having the cameras on me, but to have lost a general, a bishop and a senior TV executive for a mere half-dozen runs in less than two overs was the stuff of severe humiliation. A captain's innings was plainly required, but I could barely walk, hadn't played the game for over ten years and was never, I had to concede, much good anyway. This had all seemed such a good idea at the time. Not any more.

As I walked to the wicket the TV crew walked backwards in front of me just as they do in the real thing. This should have made me feel like Lara or Tendulkar but actually reminded me of Molesworth, that incomparably reluctant cricketer created by Geoffrey Willans and Ronald Searle. Molesworth going out to bat suddenly realises that the distance from pavilion to wicket is not 2388 miles as he originally thought but 6000.

Ed Leverton and I had, in our preparations for the game, discussed the convention of the Duke's or Duffer's run. This was something I had discovered when visiting Arundel and consulting the local score-books. The records showed that almost every time the Duke of Norfolk's Eleven played the Duke had scored a single. This was a time-honoured convention. Everyone knew that Duke Bernard was mustard-keen but not very good. To spare the ducal blushes it was therefore customary for the Duke to be given a half-volley outside the off stump or a similarly soft option. He would then put bat to ball and the fielding side would allow him to scamper down the wicket and break his duck. Thereafter they would try to get him out, invariably succeeding within the space of a very few minutes.

I asked the umpire for middle and leg. The umpire was Alexander, the elder son, which was either menacing or

reassuring. I wasn't sure which and was reminded of
Molesworth again.

'Umpire is v kind he can aford to be he hav not got to
bat.' Alexander had changed the order behind my back and
removed himself to number eleven. By the time he got in,
the match would almost certainly be all but over.

Ed, fielding at mid-on where he could control proceedings, duly explained the Duke of Norfolk convention and
the captain's free run.

Once more I was reminded of Molesworth.

Fast blower retreat with the ball muttering and cursing.
He stamp on the grass with his grate hary feet he beat
his chest and give grate cry. Then with a trumpet of
rage he charge towards you. Quake, quake ground trem-
ble birdseed fly in all directions if only you can run
away but it is not done. Grit teeth close eyes. Ball hit
your pads and everyone go mad.

Well, it wasn't going to be like that. I had the Duke's free
run. On the other hand I had to actually hit the ball somehow. I also had to hope that my wonky legs would carry me
the twenty-two yards from one end of the wicket to the
other.

Anyway, in real life Steve Arthur came in to bowl and
I duly hit the ball to gully who caught it one-handed
above his head. 'No ball,' called my number one son,
umpiring at the other end. Everybody looked mildly
amused but somewhat confused. The next ball was the
mandatory half-volley outside the off stump which I
promptly hit to mid-off but, being crippled and in pain,
forbore or forgot to run. Ed looked slightly irritated. What

was the point of offering the captain a free run if he didn't take it?

Tristram was soon out, stumped. In fact he was out stumped twice, the first time being given not out by his elder brother to the vociferous disbelief of the home team. Very next ball the same thing happened – Malcolm Roberts, the Fowey Vice-Chairman and Youth Co-ordinator, looking pretty nifty behind the stumps – by which time Alexander had been relieved at square-leg umpire by Joshi, who took a less partisan view of proceedings.

Four wickets down and we still weren't even in double figures. The camera was turning. This was awful.

It was now Neil's turn. Alexander had warned me that Neil was the one member of our team who really couldn't play cricket. He certainly didn't strike one as tremendously sporty. He had a slightly unathletic pallor, heavy stubble and he smoked. In fact he had a last gasp immediately before coming in to bat, a puff which reminded me of nothing as much as the cigarette of the condemned man about to face the firing squad.

Well, it wasn't perhaps the most cultured innings and it didn't last long, being more of a squib than an H Bomb. In fact he made 13, but this included a couple of fours and two well-struck twos which would have been at least three apiece if he hadn't been handicapped by a crippled captain who couldn't keep up with his running. Neil's main scoring stroke was what I would describe as the 'hoick', a sort of agricultural swat played with an unstraight bat across the line of the ball. It was far from being textbook or even pretty, but it was a sight more spirited than anything else we had to offer and I was very sorry when he was given out lbw. In the circumstances he should have had the benefit of the doubt, even though he was pretty plumb.

I held on for six, which could have been more if my running had been up to speed. No great shakes but still as many as our first four batsmen put together. To my slight surprise I quite enjoyed the experience and even played one shot, square off the back foot, with which I was modestly pleased. In the end, however, I was caught behind by Malcolm Roberts, with whom I'd been having a lively and probably concentration-damaging conversation. It wasn't a good shot, being a classically indecisive neither-forward-nor-back. Six wickets down and just thirty runs scored.

In that previous game at Oxford I was accused of reversing the batting order. It wasn't entirely true then and it wasn't true now. I would have said that we had four genuine batsmen and two of them were at numbers one and three. The fact that these two got just one run between them was, well, just one of those things. Funny old game.

It was also true, however, that the other two goodish batsmen were Hemish and Joshi and I'd put them in at eight and nine. My optimistic prediction would have been for the General and Bishop to produce an opening stand of between twenty and twenty-five and then to have seen Charles and Steve put on a fluent fifty or so. Then when one or other was out the survivor would have kept his wicket intact while the middle order more or less collapsed only for our face to be saved by Hemish and Joshi.

I wasn't completely out in my thinking. Our middle order, namely numbers four, five, six and seven, made 21 between them. I would just about have settled for this provided we had a hundred or so on the board by the time number four came in. In the event we had just seven.

By the time Hemish and Joshi came together it was too

late even to save a modest amount of face. Hemish made a pretty-looking 13 – the same as Neil but more cultured – but was obviously tired from his fine bowling effort. Joshi never seemed in the slightest bother but was left stranded on 23 after Joe Cox and Alexander were both out for nothing. Alexander completed the perfect symmetry of the innings by being comprehensively bowled by his very first ball, just as the General had been at the beginning of our innings. We were all out for 73.

Everyone was agreeably polite. There was much happy clapping. James Coggan appeared from the Marina Hotel with a plastic container of very strong local cider. Most of us adjourned to the upstairs bar for a beer before some of as walked down the hill to the Marina, where James and his staff laid on a delicious barbecue on the large terrace over-looking the Fowey Estuary. Ed Leverton and his wife didn't make the barbecue because he had an early train to London the following morning. By the time I arrived at the Marina it was getting dark.

'Hurry up and help yourself to food,' said David Taylor, standing with his camera and sound men. 'Now. Before the light goes.'

Did TV have any serious effect on what happened? No, I don't suppose so. I was aware of the TV team's pres-ence. Since I was wired for sound, and had to conduct interviews to camera on the field of play, it was hardly surprising if I was sometimes disconcerted. But I can't really pretend that I would have felt noticeably better or worse or even less self-conscious if it weren't for the cameras.

Nor do I think the TV seriously interfered with people's enjoyment. The pleasure of vanity being fed by the camera's attention and the pain of knowing that one's failings were being exposed to a hideously large audience probably just about cancelled each other out.

I took pleasure in one or two of the occasions I actually put bat to ball; I hated most of the fielding, remembering all too well from schooldays the strange mixture of fear, embarrassment and boredom. I took a considerable vicarious pleasure in the Bishop's bowling and Neil's batting. I particularly enjoyed Steve's stumping off the Bishop's bowling. It was also fun to see the keenness and proficiency of the younger boys – one only thirteen years old – on the other side. We of Major Rodney's were an oddly assorted collection of people – all ages and with different levels of backgrounds, skill, fitness and enthusiasm, and there was much pleasure to be had in that. The weather held up though the light was poor towards the end. The ground was beautiful. The camp-followers were entertaining and decorative, even including Kate Mortimer's boisterous sheepdog Sammy.

In the end, though, the sum was greater than the parts – and the magic of the day was elusive and indefinable. The cricket was often poor and we lost by a country mile. But never mind.

Perhaps, in a peculiar and essentially English way, that was the point.

11

Last Man In

Village cricket is alive. That much is indisputable. Alive and well? That's another matter.

Paradoxically, villages and cricket have changed more than village cricket. The sum of the two parts is not only greater than the parts, it seems more immutable. Villages are not what they were. Nor is cricket. Village cricket on the other hand survives in a form which would be readily recognisable to W.G. Grace and his brothers or the Revd Vere Dashwood of North Perrot and Prebendary Wickham of Martock. The latter two would surely make common cause with the present-day Revd Jack Wixon of Wrea Green. I'm pretty sure too that Sir John Squire would hit it off with Ben Brocklehurst and that Sir Dennis Boles could be beamed down from heaven and open the batting at Bishops Lydeard with only a flutter of unfamiliarity.

'And is there honey still for tea?' Well, yes, actually. And a good strong, sweet brew from the same huge tin or enamel teapots they'd have used a hundred years ago or even earlier.

The changing face of the English village itself, however, has been the subject of dismay since Oliver Goldsmith wrote 'The Deserted Village' in 1770.

'These were thy charms, sweet village,' lamented Goldsmith, '. . . but all these charms are fled.'

Sweet smiling village, loveliest of the lawn,
Thy sports are fled, and all thy charms withdrawn.

Bearing in mind that this was the time when that most remarkable of historic village teams, Hampshire's Hambledon, was at its peak, you could be forgiven for thinking that the poet was being unduly pessimistic. Almost two hundred years later, Agatha Christie's redoubtable Miss Marple, resident in arguably the most idyllic English village ever, said of St Mary Mead, 'It used to be a very pretty old-world village but of course like everything else it's becoming what they call "developed" these days.'

People like Goldsmith and Miss Marple are still wringing their hands over what has happened to our villages. The decline and fall of the English village has been a constant refrain for hundreds of years and particularly in the time since village cricket assumed a more or less recognisable form at the end of the nineteenth century. We all know the symptoms. The Church has sold the old vicarage and one man is now ministering to perhaps half a dozen villages. The ancient squirearchical family, cruelly depleted by two world wars and financially crippled by death duties and the decline of traditional agriculture, have long since sold up and vanished. The shop's gone. There's a new housing estate on the outskirts of the village. Many of the new incomers commute to London or the nearest big city. The school has closed. There is a mobile telephone mast in a prominent beauty spot and the council houses sport TV dishes. The bus service is terrible and the bus-shelter has been vandalised and disfigured by graffiti. And so on.

You can't dispute that these things have happened in a great many rural communities. Yet they are not universal and they have not necessarily destroyed the cricket.

The changes in cricket itself, as observed on television and reported in papers and magazines, are just as radical. The game at the professional level is infinitely more commercial, with television and sponsorhip ubiquitous and dominant. Advertising hoardings have even trickled down to the grass roots, disfiguring even such remote spots as the green field at Werrington just west of the Tamar valley and the beautiful views of Dartmoor in the distance.

Television itself with its instant replays, technical analysis and constant close-ups has dramatically changed the way we watch the game. It has demystified it, brought a measure of understanding even to the most ignorant couch-potato and, in the process of demystifying the game, removed some of the romance, the magic and the mystery.

The abolition of the distinction between Gentlemen and Players, aka amateurs and professionals, took place in 1963, and the professional and commercial nature of the game at the top level was confirmed by the intervention of the Australian TV magnate Kerry Packer in the late seventies. The social inequalities of the old Gents and Players era, with the two classes of player emerging on to the field of play through different gates, travelling in different railway carriages and staying at separate hotels, was plainly preposterous. Modernists, such as the late Sir Derek Birley, author of an award-winning social history of English cricket, are sometimes a shade too scornful about the influence of the old-guard amateurs. You could argue that I am biased, as the biographer of Denis Compton and Brian Johnston, though the point, much missed, about both men is that they were consummate paid professionals who nevertheless played the game and commented on it in a Corinthian, joyful manner which has, perhaps misleadingly, been identified with amateurism. Plenty of the old amateurs played cricket in a dour, grudging spirit and their enemies would argue that famous amateurs such as W.G. Grace and D.R. Jardine were really 'shamateurs' who made money from the game and were not above a spot of sharp practice or even cheating. Many of those who played the game for a living lifted the hearts by the exuberance of their play, none more so than those champions of different generations – Denis Compton and Ian Botham.

Nonetheless and notwithstanding, what is still, oddly, identified as 'first-class' cricket does seem to have become a duller game in its completely commercial and professional form. No one could countenance a return to the old days, but most people who have lived in both eras would surely agree that at the top level cricket seems to have become more of a job than a joy.

The fact that village cricket is still, on the whole and with relatively minor reservations, played for fun and for its own sake, makes it diverse, entertaining, odd and unpredictable. Naturally the game at this level reflects the changes that have taken place in cricket at the level of commercial entertainment (which is what the first-class game has become), just as it reflects the changes that have taken place in the social and physical fabric of the English village.

On the whole, however, the spirit and traditions of English village cricket have survived with remarkable vigour. The Cornish club dinner where I was invited to speak and where Mrs Heald drew the raffle tickets and which started my musings on the subject of village cricket has turned out to contain a number of universal truths.

There are still, in England, budding youngsters, loyal tea ladies, beaming farmers, supportive gentry and even cricketing clergy. Nor are they confined to somnolent communities in the rural South. They crop up everywhere. I could argue that the further a village is from a big city the more likely it is to have a cricket club which is at the very heart of the social fabric of the place, but although there are wonderfully sociable cricket clubs at what in English terms counts as the far ends of the earth, there are equally attractive clubs in suburbs and stockbroker belts.

They come and they go. In some cases when they go they go for ever, but dead clubs are surprisingly often reborn. Villages have changed and cricket has changed, but village cricket has changed less than either.

The most contentious issue in village cricket is the question of skill and competition. Should it be skilful and competitive or not? There are those who believe that the grass-roots game should be the base of a pyramid of excellence which leads inexorably to a world-beating national team. For this to happen standards have to be as high as possible in all

respects, there should be numerous nets and fielding practices, sobriety at all times and an eagerness to achieve victory
which might even come at all costs, including sledging and,
not to put too fine a point on it, cheating.

There are others who believe that village cricket is an end
in itself and that standards of play are little more than inci-
dental. This school of thought has it that the inclusion of at
least one complete duffer is an essential part of any team,
and even that rules and regulations should be made up – by
agreement of the two captains and umpires – more or less
as you go along. Real cricketing Luddites almost believe that
a certain cricketing hopelessness and *laissez-faire* is essential
to the village game.

My own prejudices favour enthusiasm over competence.
My earliest experiences of the game were *The Pickwick Papers*,
England, their England and the Fulmer Wreck and Creation
Ground. There were, in all three, elements of genuine prowess.
Bobby Southcott aka Alec Waugh was obviously a very
elegant and accomplished player by almost any standard. His
captain, Mr Hodge or Sir John Squire, equally evidently wasn't.
But the game, in my estimation, is incomparably enriched
by the Squires and Hodges, not least because on the village
cricket ground the playing field is level and the oddest things
happen.

Jeremy Paul, the script-writer and playwright, who wrote
the history of the Invalids and is or more accurately *was* a
very handy player, told me a story of how in a charity match
he once opened the batting with a youthful Viv Richards
and scored fifty. Better still was his fielding, for standing at
slip he caught the England opener, John Edrich, almost before
he had opened his account. It was, according to Jeremy, a
stupendous catch and I believe him.

Later that season Edrich battled away against a formidable West Indian attack and made hundreds of famous runs. When the season was over he bumped into one of the men who had been playing in the charity match with Jeremy Paul. The man congratulated Edrich on his brilliant first-class season, but the great man wasn't interested. Instead he asked, crossly, 'Who was that tall bugger who caught me at slip?'

This sort of story represents the magic of village cricket. It is, or should be, a stage on which, just once or twice in a lifetime, a modest talent shines forth and excels itself, preferably at the expense of one infinitely more gifted and successful. Village cricket, at its best, is a mingling of abilities as well as of age and class and wealth and race and everything else it's possible to mix. (I wish there were more women playing the game, as an element of male chauvinism has always been one of the game's less attractive elements.) Cricket at the top is no longer the great leveller identified by G.M. Trevelyan. Cricket at the grass roots – village cricket – is still a leveller.

In the north of England clubs have tended to be organised in competitive leagues since at least the last quarter of the nineteenth century. In the South the leagues came later but they are now effectively universal. This has meant that grass-roots cricket has become a more serious affair with a bureaucratic element that I don't much like. Anonymous blazers now tell historic clubs that they have to have sight-screens, covered offices for scorers, changing-rooms for umpires and new balls for every innings. The same blazers dictate the number of overs and impose those incomprehensible Duckworth-Lewis rules to settle the scores in the event of the cricketing equivalent of leaves on the line or the wrong sort of snow. Paradoxically the blazers have allowed a tip-and-run game of twenty overs a side for TV and money at the 'top' end while insisting that down in the basement league cricketers must grind out games of forty or more overs a side on the grounds that only this is a preparation for the realities of the higher grades of cricket. Surely some mistake?

I see the logic of the leagues, and in many ways they have been a force for good and an instrument of survival. On the other hand they threaten the spirit of anarchy and independence which I believe is fundamental to village cricket. They have, without meaning to, encouraged 'sledging' and foul play and they have made it difficult for wandering social sides and their ilk to find fixtures. They are also, often, in conflict with the Village Cup. This seems ridiculous, for the leagues and the Village Cup fit together as attractively as the Football League and the FA Cup in Association Football. In cricket I think I see the greater chances of the unexpected upset, which is a characteristic of the cup, as being more in the spirit of the village game. It would certainly be a shame if the dominance of the leagues were to kill off the cup.

Despite all that has happened, sides such as Major Rodney's still flourish. Well, in the case of my team which has played just two matches in over a decade of existence 'flourish' may be a self-deluding word. 'Flourish' I think we do, in an admittedly spasmodic manner, but the league structure is not on our side. 'League cricket is God,' Michael Williams, the founder of the Cornish Crusaders, remarked to me somewhat ruefully.

Leagues have improved the quality of play in village cricket and this is widely perceived as being 'a good thing'.

I am less than wholly convinced about this.

If something is worth doing, it's worth doing badly. And of nothing is this more true than cricket. And nowhere is it more appropriate to play cricket badly than on the village green. It matters not who won or lost but how you played the game. Actually how you played the game doesn't matter that much either. It's more a question of taking part and entering into the spirit of the thing.

Village cricket in its purest form does not aspire to supreme excellence. It would be perverse to argue that the fewer the skills the better the game, but you know, or should know, what I mean. The true spirit of this game lies elsewhere. One of the great moments in my memories of cricket at any level is bringing the Bishop of Truro back to bowl from the Hall end and watching him get one past the Chairman of Fowey's immaculate forward defensive and have him stumped by the Head of Programmes at Carlton Television. That's my idea of perfect cricket and of village cricket at its best.

As long as it's fun nothing else really matters.

Index

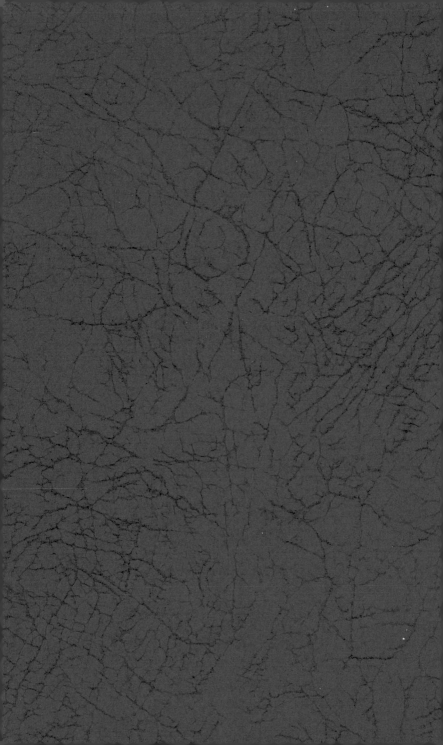